"Some Appointed Work To Do"

**Recent Titles in
Contributions in Women's Studies**

Women, Community, and the Hormel Strike of 1985–86
Neala J. Schleuning

Edith Wharton's Prisoners of Consciousness: A Study of Theme and Technique
in the Tales
Evelyn E. Fracasso

Mothers and Work in Popular American Magazines
Kathryn Keller

Ideals in Feminine Beauty: Philosophical, Social, and Cultural Dimensions
Karen A. Callaghan, editor

The Stone and the Scorpion: The Female Subject of Desire in the Novels of Charlotte
Brontë, George Eliot, and Thomas Hardy
Judith Mitchell

The Several Worlds of Pearl S. Buck: Essays Presented at a Centennial Symposium,
Randolph-Macon Woman's College, March 26–28, 1992
Elizabeth J. Lipscomb, Frances E. Webb, and Peter Conn, editors

Hear Me Patiently: The Reform Speeches of Amelia Jenks Bloomer
Anne C. Coon, editor

Nineteenth-Century American Women Theatre Managers
Jane Kathleen Curry

Textual Escap(e)ades: Mobility, Maternity, and Textuality in Contemporary Fiction
by Women
Lindsey Tucker

The Repair of the World: The Novels of Marge Piercy
Kerstin W. Shands

Clara Barton: In the Service of Humanity
David H. Burton

International Women's Writing: New Landscapes of Identity
Anne E. Brown and Marjanne Goozé, editors

"Some Appointed Work To Do"

Women and Vocation in the Fiction of Elizabeth Gaskell

Robin B. Colby

Contributions in Women's Studies, Number 150

GREENWOOD PRESS
Westport, Connecticut • London

Library of Congress Cataloging-in-Publication Data

Colby, Robin B.
    Some appointed work to do : women and vocation in the fiction of
Elizabeth Gaskell / Robin B. Colby.
        p.   cm.—(Contributions in women's studies, ISSN 0147–104X ;
no. 150)
    Includes bibliographical references and index.
    ISBN 0–313–29373–2
    1. Gaskell, Elizabeth Cleghorn, 1810–1865—Characters—Women.
2. Feminism and literature—England—History—19th century.
3. Women and literature—England—History—19th century. 4. Women—
Employment—England—History—19th century. 5. Vocation in
literature. 6. Work in literature.   I. Title.   II. Series.
PR4711.C65 1995
823'.8—dc20   94–46946

British Library Cataloguing in Publication Data is available.

Library of Congress Catalog Card Number: 94–46946
ISBN: 0–313–29373–2
ISSN: 0147–104X

First published in 1995

Greenwood Press, 88 Post Road West, Westport, CT 06881
An imprint of Greenwood Publishing Group, Inc.

Printed in the United States of America

The paper used in this book complies with the
Permanent Paper Standard issued by the National
Information Standards Organization (Z39.48–1984).

10 9 8 7 6 5 4 3 2 1

Copyright Acknowledgment

The Letters of Mrs. Gaskell, edited by J.A.V. Chapple and Arthur Pollard
(Manchester University Press: 1967) are excerpted by permission of the publisher.

This book is dedicated to Jane Tompkins, whose course in American Women Writers inspired many of the ideas here and whose advice and encouragement strengthened me to do the work.

Contents

Acknowledgments

As I have worked on this project, I have been helped by many people. First, I wish to thank my parents and my sister for their love and confidence in me. For his quiet understanding and patience, I am grateful to my husband, Paul, who probably knew best of all how important writing this book has been to me. My gratitude goes also to Clyde de L. Ryals, who directed my dissertation and whose insightful comments rang in my head as I revised it into its current form. I am grateful to Ann Newman, of Greenwood Press, for her technical expertise and her unfailing cheerfulness as she answered my questions. I am also appreciative of the friendship and support of my colleagues at Meredith College. To Pam Bencke and Allyson Swelam, for the time and care spent getting the manuscript in final form, I want to express my heartfelt thanks. And finally to Matthew, Megan, and Gray, thank you for making my heart light.

"Some Appointed Work To Do"

Chapter 1

Introduction

In a much-quoted essay, Jane Tompkins has defended Harriet Beecher Stowe against charges of sentimentality and conservatism by arguing that Stowe attempted in her fiction to "reorganize culture from the woman's point of view" and to offer a "critique of American society."[1] In her analysis of *Uncle Tom's Cabin*, Tompkins convincingly demonstrates how Stowe's seemingly conventional vision, which affirms motherhood, home, family, and religion, is in fact revolutionary because it attempts to shift the center of power in American life, "placing it not in the government, nor in the courts of law, nor in the factories, nor in the marketplace, but in the kitchen." In the kitchen "mothers and grandmothers do the world's primary work," while men, whose actions Carlyle believed constituted human history, are removed to the periphery. This shift, Tompkins claims, is the most radical feature of Stowe's "millenarian scheme."

A similar case could be made for Elizabeth Gaskell. Like Stowe, Gaskell has been long underestimated. Perceived by David Cecil as the "typical Victorian lady," "all a woman was expected to be," Gaskell has not always been taken as seriously as she deserves.[2] Almost as well received in her day as Charles Dickens, Gaskell has not maintained the reputation that Dickens has. Indeed, she has been misrepresented as docile and submissive by critics like Cecil, who believe that "so far from chafing at the limits imposed on her activities, she accepted them with serene satisfaction." Even recent critics see Gaskell as limited by conventionality and by a religious orientation.[3] She has been represented as a conservative writer who unquestioningly embraces received ideas about the dominant ideology of gender. Yet, given the constraints of Victorian culture, Gaskell's novels may in fact be seen as radical because they challenge widely held assumptions about the nature of women, their proper sphere, and their participation in labor. Gaskell's treatment of work, in particular, is revealing, for it can serve as a testing ground for her attitudes and purposes. Work, after all, is a site where the dominant ideology operates as it encodes separate roles for men and women. By examining the theme of women's labor in Gaskell's fiction, I will show dimensions in her thinking and art that have not been fully recognized by the critics.

Gaskell lived in a century that was riddled with change; her fiction is in many ways a response to changes that were occurring in her lifetime and at the same time is an agent of change. Capitalizing on her respectable status as the wife of a minister and mother of four, Gaskell entered the Condition of England debate to make new claims for women.

This debate was in part a response to industrialization and its dramatic effects on the organization of labor. Some contemporary social commentators, most notably Macaulay, approved of the economic changes that were taking place. In his review essay on *Southey's Colloquies*, Macaulay alluded to the signs of the natural progress of society: "We see the wealth of nations increasing, and all the arts of life approaching nearer and nearer to perfection."[4] Although not all observers agreed that England was nearing perfection, this largely agrarian nation in which the primary unit of production had been the household was nonetheless rapidly becoming a nation of factories, which represented for many the power and force of the industrial world.

Numerous Victorians evinced great enthusiasm for the mechanization of England. To some thinkers of the period, machinery represented a boundless capacity for work. The Victorians have repeatedly been associated with energy and a commitment to the work ethic. In the discourse on labor that formed a part of the Condition of England debate, a variety of figures took positions on the issue of work, especially on working women. Mary Poovey has suggested that the middle-class ideology associated with the Victorians was continually "in the making," "open to revision, dispute, and the emergence of oppositional formulations."[5] Specifically, Poovey concludes that the development of a set of ideas about gender was what she calls "uneven"; that is, it was experienced differently by different individuals as well as articulated differently by different spokespersons. Poovey's thesis is useful, for it explains how there was room for dissenting voices within a dominant ideology of womanhood. I wish to show that Elizabeth Gaskell was one dissenting voice.

For the Victorians, work was ideologically linked with virtue. Deeply rooted in the middle class, the Anglo-American work ethic was clearly articulated by a group including such culturally influential figures as Isaac Watts, Benjamin Franklin, Thomas Carlyle, and Samuel Smiles. The work ethic involved an unquestioning faith in action and a disdain for idleness. It was inculcated early as, even from the cradle, children were accustomed to hearing maxims affirming the dignity of labor. One of the most pervasive images of labor comes from Isaac Watts: "How doth the little busy bee/Improve each shining hour,/And gather honey all the day/From every opening flower!" (*Divine Songs*). Franklin likewise emphasized the importance of steady labor; in Poor

Richard's words, "God gives all things to Industry." Other aphorisms, on the other hand, were cautionary, emphasizing the consequences of a lack of occupation: "For Satan finds some mischief still/For idle hands to do" (Watts, *Divine Songs*, XX).

The rhetoric of work in the nineteenth century consistently characterized labor as a positive activity. Carlyle declared, "All work, even cotton spinning, is noble."[6] Work was, for Carlyle, of a religious nature: "In all true Work, were it but true hand-labour, there is something of divineness. Labour, wide as the Earth, has its summit in Heaven."[7] Indeed, as Carlyle saw it, work issued from the creative principle: "Labour is Life: from the inmost heart of the Worker rises his God-given Force, the sacred celestial Life-essence breathed into him by Almighty God."[8] Conversely, leisure was associated with moral weakness. Part of the reason for such a view stems from a Protestant fear of luxury, leisure, and ease.

The nineteenth-century attitude contrasts sharply with a much older view of work. The Victorians had come a long way from Aristotle's claim that the most appropriate life for man was a life of leisure. In fact, throughout Western history, a man's immunity from labor was a mark of his high social status. To be genteel meant to be leisured. In the golden age poets affirmed the joys of leisure. In the Judeo-Christian tradition, the biblical narrative included as a condition of the fall the prospect of endless labor. In the Middle Ages, the highest ideal was a life of contemplation and prayer. However, with the Protestant Reformation, men were set to work in the world and to shun idleness, for time on earth had to be accounted for in heaven.[9]

Following in this Protestant tradition, the Victorians were energetic spokespersons for the sanctity of labor. Exalted conceptions of work were useful to the Victorians for a number of reasons. The kind of intensity with which the Utilitarians threw themselves into social projects did not leave much room for self-examination; too much speculation could lead to paralysis. In an age when scientific discoveries were shaking long-held assumptions and beliefs, it was thought that work helped banish the "sick fatigue," the "languid doubt" that Arnold saw as typical of his generation (Scholar-Gypsy, 1. 164). In particular, unsettling revelations about the evolution of man made it necessary for the Victorians to affirm their superiority over other species. Work kept the animal instincts in check. Tennyson's speaker in "Locksley Hall" knows the perils of inaction: "I myself must mix with action, lest I wither in despair" (1. 98). Moreover, in an industrial economy, work was viewed as the key to success, requiring the capitalist virtues of endurance, self-restraint, and persistence. Ultimately, for the Victorians work was a means of expressing the self. "A small Poet every Worker is," said Carlyle.[10] In work, both mind and spirit played a part, transforming mechanical labor into a kind of art. To work was to create.

Discussions of work during the Victorian period proceeded under the assumption that the worker is male: Carlyle wrote, "Blessed is he who has found his work"; "Know what thou canst work at; and work at it, like a Hercules!" Carlyle links true work with masculine power as he invokes an image of a workforce "heaving, struggling, all shoulders at the wheel; their heart pulsing, every muscle swelling, with man's energy and will . . . warriors in the one true war."[11] Ford Madox Brown's *Work* (1852-65) draws on the same image: a group of navvies, or excavators, appears in the center of the canvas, surrounded by, or plying, their tools. The masculine vigor of the workmen is heightened by the contrasting image of two well-dressed ladies carefully making their way along the periphery of the scene. Throughout the period, work was associated with masculinity, aggression, the life force itself.

The identification of labor with the masculine failed to acknowledge the actual participation of women in the labor force.[12] Within the factories, in increasing numbers, were female workers. According to the 1851 Census, 140,000 women over twenty were employed in domestic service, 125,000 in clothing and shoemaking, 11,000 in teaching, 9,000 in the silk industry, and the remainder in other branches of manufacture.[13] Because they were held mainly by women, these occupations yielded low wages and little prestige. More hidden was the labor that women performed inside the home. Not surprisingly, the issue of women's work became a topic that sparked much passionate discussion, both among the leading feminists of the day and among those who saw the feminization of the labor force as a sign of the nation's degeneration.[14] Thus the "Condition of England" debate raised the "Woman Question." The "Woman Question," with which midcentury Victorians were preoccupied, centered upon woman's proper sphere.

While for men waged work was essential to moral and financial success, for women it was corrupting; it tainted and sullied.[15] The Victorians believed that work outside the home interfered with the natural roles of women: wifehood and motherhood. According to domestic ideology, women need seek no further than these roles for their life's purpose: being a wife or being a mother *was itself* a vocation.[16] However, domestic ideology was clearly at odds with actual social conditions and social trends: the 1851 Census revealed that 42 percent of women between the ages of twenty and forty were unmarried and that two million out of Britain's six million supported themselves.[17] Large numbers of women, then, were not finding their vocation in home and family. Nevertheless both men and women found the new trends disconcerting and spoke out against women's participation in the labor force. W. R. Greg's 1862 essay called "Why are Women Redundant" is a frequently cited expression of the position that women's natural role was to be wives and mothers.[18] One of the most insistent spokespersons for this ideology of domesticity, Sarah Ellis wrote in *The Women of England* (1835), "The sphere of woman's happiest and most beneficial influence is a domestic one."[19] According to Ellis, woman's truest work involved self-denial, self-sacrifice, and complete dedication to the family unit.

While men's work met with social approval, women's participation in the workforce was often viewed as the source of social problems, particularly the degeneration of the family.

The idealization of women in the nineteenth century, articulated perhaps most memorably by Coventry Patmore in "The Angel in the House," separated women from work in representation, but not in fact. Julia Swindell points out that capitalism required that women *not be* separated from the workforce.[20] Workers of all kinds were needed to fulfill the growing demands of an increasingly industrial economy. At the same time, nineteenth-century ideology proclaimed the incompatibility of women and a professional career, ignoring the great—and growing—numbers of women in place in the workforce. The effect of such an ideology, Swindell concludes, was not to separate women from the workplace, but to separate them from power.

Proponents of domestic ideology like Sarah Ellis and John Ruskin argued that the confinement of women within the home was necessary if they were to perform their civilizing function.[21] Home was to be a haven, a refuge from the capitalist workplace. In "Of Queens' Gardens," Ruskin asserted that while man "in his rough work in open world, must encounter all peril and trial," women are guarded from all such experiences: "within his house, as ruled by her, unless she herself has sought it, need enter no danger, no temptation, no cause of error or offense."[22] Woman's proper vocation, as Ruskin saw it, is to adorn the home, "the place of Peace." As for her social function, Ruskin wrote, "the woman's duty, as a member of the commonwealth, is to assist in the ordering, in the comforting, and in the beautiful adornment of the state." To that end she should be educated: "all such knowledge should be given her as may enable her to understand, and even to aid, the work of men." Sarah Ellis likewise saw women's function as assisting "their brothers, their husbands, or their sons in becoming happier and better men."[23]

Tennyson's *The Princess* (1847) takes a more progressive view, although its own revolutionary rhetoric does not control the poem through and through. Having been introduced to theories of equality by two widows, Princess Ida founds a university for women, where men are strictly forbidden. When the prince, to whom Ida has been betrothed from childhood, sneaks into her kingdom in disguise in order to claim his fiancée, he is discovered and a war erupts. The princess and the prince eventually fall in love, sharing in a dream of equality for the future.

On the surface the poem challenges Victorian concepts of gender. The prince is described in terms of gentleness and beauty while Princess Ida is described as a powerful leader. Moreover, the prince makes some extraordinary speeches, claiming that "The woman's cause is man's; they rise or sink/Together" (7.243-4). He offers to join with Ida in her cause, telling her "Work no more alone!" and promising,

> We two will serve them both in aiding her—
> Will clear away the parasitic forms
> That seem to keep her up but drag her down—
> Will leave her space to burgeon out of all
> Within her—let her make herself her own
> To give or keep, to live and learn and be
> All that not harms distinctive womanhood.
> For woman is not undevelopt man,
> But diverse. (7.249, 252-60)

The prince's ideal is one of androgyny: "The man be more of woman, she of man" (7.264). The end of the poem leaves the couple looking hopefully toward the promise of a new day.

However, the language of the poem is not always consistent with the liberating vision articulated in these speeches. For example, the poem associates femininity with service, implying that women are most truly womanly when they are ministering to men. At first Ida is inflexible about the infiltration of men into her terrain, but after she sees all the casualties of war, she is moved to open the doors of her palace. The women begin to tend the wounded, and are feminized:

> The maidens came, they talk'd,
> They sang, they read; till she not fair began
> To gather light, and she that was became
> Her former beauty treble; and to and fro
> With books, with flowers, with angel offices,
> Like creatures native unto gracious act,
> And in their own clear element, they moved. (7.7-10)

The language here suggests that women are in their "clear element" when they are performing "angel offices." Although the poem has established the intellectual accomplishments possessed by the women at the university, in this scene they drop their studies, offering their books to cheer their patients. Likewise, when Princess Ida begins to fall in love with the prince, and, at his dying request, kisses him, she is transformed:

> The bosom with long sighs labor'd; and meek
> Seem'd the full lips, and mild the luminous eyes,
> And the voice trembled and the hand. She said
> Brokenly, that she knew it, she had fail'd
> In sweet humility, had fail'd in all. (7.210-14)

Many of the words in this passage emphasize weakness: "meek," "mild," "trembled," "brokenly," "humility." The poem indicates that Princess Ida becomes a woman when she puts aside her lofty ideals and allows herself to enter into conventional feminine experience. The implication is that woman's natural vocation is love.

The Victorian notion that women are best suited for courtship and marriage is likewise reflected in the art of the period.[24] The images of little girls in Victorian art reveal the restrictions that circumscribed female lives from childhood. Sophie Anderson's *No Walk Today* (mid-1850s) is one such example. In this painting a doll-like child is prevented from going outside. The image of an elaborately dressed girl, standing at a window, implies the kind of narrow existence that the future will hold for the woman she will become.[25] Arranged to be merely an object of admiration, the child looks wistfully beyond her boundaries. The picture *Childhood* (1855) by James Collinson portrays two sisters, the older playing mother to the younger. With her hair put up, the oldest sister, still a young girl, steps into the role that has been prescribed for her. William Maw Egley's *Just as the Twig is Bent* (1861) depicts two little girls and one boy, who is dressed as a soldier. The two girls are seated at a table while the boy is standing, in a military posture. Fascinated, the girls turn from their books to watch the boy's antics. This painting likewise communicates in miniature what life will hold for the three children: the boy has access to the active life, while the girls must wait on the sidelines until they are chosen to be wives.

Not surprisingly, many representations of women in Victorian art centered upon their roles in courtship and marriage. In these romantic scenes, women get center stage; clearly, courtship is their acknowledged domain, the principal drama of their lives. Once courtship was over, motherhood followed. The image of woman as wife and mother is ubiquitous in Victorian art. *Woman's Mission: Companion to Manhood* (1863) by George Elgar Hicks calls up the image of woman as helpmate. In this painting the husband is distressed by the news contained in a letter he is holding in his hand. The wife, ever ready with emotional support, offers consolation as she clings to his arm. The breakfast things, the well-furnished room, and her own neat dress all point to the domestic talents of the wife. Charles W. Cope's *Life Well Spent* (1862) depicts a model mother surrounded by her children. As she listens to her sons' lessons, the mother knits. Following her mother's example, the daughter rocks the cradle of the baby with one hand, using the other to hold her book. This tableau of quiet industry commends the exemplary mother for attending zealously to her household. *Quiet* (1860) by William Nicol is a similar work extolling maternal care. A smiling mother sits with her child, content with her domestic role. A book in her lap suggests that she diligently fulfills her motherly duties.

Although such idealized images of womanly perfection are prevalent, Victorian art also portrayed the erring wife (*Past and Present*, 1858, Augustus Egg) and the neglectful mother (*Time Ill Spent*, 1862?, Charles W. Cope). Whether they were exemplars or cautionary examples, images of Victorian women most frequently derived from their positions as wives and mothers.

Though not completely absent, images of women as workers were more rare. Only a few paintings of the mid-1800s treat the subject of female labor. And when women are portrayed as workers, their work more often than not is presented as dispiriting, demoralizing. Paintings like Richard Redgrave's *Going into Service* (1843) and *The Sempstress* (1846) represent labor as a last resort. In the first work, a young girl reluctantly faces the prospect of leaving home to help support her family. In the second, a gaunt young seamstress looks toward heaven, as if asking for release from the exhausting routine which is her life. Similarly, Redgrave's *The Poor Teacher* (1845) emphasizes the trials of being a governess: a lone figure sits in her empty schoolroom, her drooping head evidence of her low spirits.

Popular fiction during the Victorian period took a similar stance toward working women. Writers frequently represented women's victimization as resulting from their work. Charlotte Elizabeth Tonna in *The Forsaken Home* created the picture of an exploited family in which the mother is employed as a machine operative at low wages. She attempts to support her family, but her husband becomes a drunkard and her children are neglected. The mother, not the father, is held responsible for these failures. Tonna took the details in her stories from the Blue Books, which documented the squalor that often accompanied employment for women. Similarly, the victims of the sweat shops, especially the seamstresses, are evoked in popular fiction of the time as pathetic figures of oppression.

The subject of work for women was particularly relevant for women writers, who experienced personal conflicts as a result of their desire to be viewed both as domestic and womanly and of their need as artists to assert themselves in the performance of work. Charlotte Brontë focuses on this conflict in the partly autobiographical *Jane Eyre* (1847). After Jane leaves Mr. Rochester, she is forced to seek work. Because she is a woman, only a limited number of options are available to her. She tells St. John Rivers, "I will be a dressmaker; I will be a plain-workwoman; I will be a servant, a nurse-girl, if I can be no better."[26] When she is offered the post of village schoolmistress, she accepts, realizing that it is the best among several unsatisfactory choices. However, such work—though somewhat socially acceptable since she has no one to support her—is not fulfilling for the unmarried Jane; after a "day passed in honorable exertion," she experiences "strange dreams at night: dreams many-coloured, agitated, full of the ideal, the stirring, the stormy." The kind of work that is accessible to Jane does not give full play to her talents and faculties.

Likewise, in Brontë's *Villette* (1853), Lucy Snowe, faced with the necessity of supporting herself, resolves to become a governess, taking the attitude "I had nothing to lose."[27] For Lucy, "work had neither charm for [her] taste, nor hold on [her] interest." Like Jane, she yearns for stimulus: "I did long, achingly, . . . for something to fetch me out of my present existence, and lead me upwards and onwards." In both cases, what the women desire—scope for their abilities—is not socially acceptable for them to pursue. For Brontë, womanly and artistic duties were perpetually in conflict. For her characters, work, in the sense of an activity that earns daily bread, is at odds with vocation, an inclination or calling that brings intellectual and emotional gratification. Brontë's novels emphasize the waste of female potential.

Maggie Tulliver in Eliot's *The Mill on the Floss* (1860) yearns vaguely for purpose and action. Much more intelligent than her brother Tom—it is she who helps him with Latin—Maggie is nevertheless shut out from the occupations that he is expected to pursue. Given the advantage of an education that is really beyond his ken, Tom sets concrete goals and works hard to achieve them. Maggie, on the other hand, is neglected, her intellect and imagination largely wasted in a sterile environment, her powers channeled solely into a longing for love.

Similarly, Dorothea in *Middlemarch* (1872) is denied the fulfillment of useful, independent work. Her first marriage, to the pedant Causabon, stifles her talents as she defers to her husband's sense of his own great calling. Her second marriage, though more personally fulfilling, also fails to provide an adequate outlet for her abilities. The most she can hope for herself is "to help someone who did great works."[28] For Dorothea, there is the "feeling that there was always something better which she might have done, if she had only been better and known better."

In *Writing beyond the Ending* Rachel Du Plessis points out the dilemma of the Victorian woman in a culture that severely limits her choices: lacking serious options in work or vocation, she must define herself through romantic choice. As Du Plessis sees it, there were only two rightful endings of nineteenth-century novels about women: successful courtship and marriage, or death, both of which are resolutions of romance. While for men the quest ending (*Bildungsroman*) and the romance ending are *both* possible, for the heroine the two cannot easily coexist. Du Plessis argues that one part of the alternate endings, usually quest, is "set aside or repressed, whether by marriage or death."[29] Victorian society defined "work" very narrowly for women: their task—their true vocation—was to acquire a husband and produce a family. The search for an independent purpose, for a life's work, which was such an important part of masculine self-definition, was socially unacceptable for women. Women artists who were not satisfied with the narrow boundaries of experience prescribed for women either expressed in their fiction the frustration of being denied the opportunity of defining one's own work, or, more rarely, offered an alternative view of the importance of a new kind of vocation for women.

Against this background Elizabeth Gaskell wrote fiction that wrestled with the issue of women's work. Françoise Basch observes that Gaskell is the only one among the major writers of the first half of the Victorian period to have dealt rather fully with the subject.[30]   She goes on to point out that Gaskell is interested in all kinds of occupations, those held by middle-class girls as well as those held by working women.   Perhaps because she was the mother of four daughters—two of whom never married—Gaskell was particularly sensitive to the plight of unmarried women, whose identities could not be shaped by their roles as wives or mothers and who consequently needed to acquire self-definition through other means.   Yet even Basch devotes only a few pages to Gaskell, despite her argument that Gaskell stands out among novelists of her time in her treatment of the subject of work and women.   Unlike many other women writers who portray female characters as victims, Gaskell confers upon her characters a measure of control over the circumstances of their lives.[31]   Judith Newton has argued that women novelists like Austen, Brontë, and Eliot have sometimes subverted masculine domination by giving emphasis to female capability.[32] According to Newton, this "power of ability or capability" can be defined as "achievement and competence, and by implication, as a form of self-definition or self-rule."   In this sense, Gaskell is interested in presenting her female characters as powerful; by exploring the process by which they *choose* a direction for their lives, Gaskell links women's work with their empowerment.

Coming to Gaskell at the end of the twentieth century is both necessary and instructive, for the question of the role that work plays in a woman's life is still problematic.[33]   In her life, as well as in her fiction, Gaskell was interested in creating arrangements that would make it possible for women to have marriage and family, as well as some sort of separate vocation.   And, despite the unconventional nature of Gaskell's proposal, she was extremely successful in "having it all" in an era that did not recognize women's need for an identity separate from their roles in the family.   What is remarkable about Gaskell is that she managed to maintain both a respectable public image as a devoted Victorian wife and mother and to create a surprisingly modern household in which it was possible for her to pursue her chosen vocation of writing.   Most important, she dared to suggest fulfilling possibilities for women that her culture had not imagined.

Gaskell's particular advantages as an upper middle-class woman, as well as her personal skill in turning her personal circumstances to her own advantage, enabled her to write.   Fortunate in her family connections, she had both an aunt and a father who instructed and encouraged her in her work.   Moreover, her educational experiences and the perspectives she absorbed from her Unitarian training gave her the confidence in her own gifts that she needed in order to attempt writing.   Once married, she received support from her husband, her daughters, and her servants.   In her study of feminist lives in Victorian England, Philippa Levine notes that marriage did not often lead the early feminists to abandon their views; instead, they sought marital arrangements that would allow them to pursue their own goals and projects.[34]   Therefore marriage could in fact provide a kind of freedom within which they could work.   Gaskell was smart enough to choose a mate who would further—not hinder—her writing career. An extraordinary manager, she also used her organizational skills to create the kind of household in which it was possible for her to write. Interruptions were a constant problem, but at the same time, she drew on the experiences of her crowded life as sources for her writing, often taking as her subject the problems of women.[35] Despite the complexities of her life, she attained a popularity and a reputation that rivaled Dickens', a remarkable accomplishment for a mother of four who wrote in a time when motherhood itself was viewed as requiring all of a woman's attention and energy.

The family background out of which Gaskell developed helped form her attitudes toward womanly potential. When Gaskell's mother died, she was sent to Knutsford to live with her mother's unmarried sister, Hannah Lumb. Patsy Stoneman suggests that the aunt served not only as an excellent mother-substitute but also as an important role model, showing Gaskell that a woman could live an independent and satisfying life. Gaskell grew up in a household of females, a household for all practical purposes headed by a competent single mother. Exposed early to female authority, she saw in her aunt an able, self-sufficient woman, who was capable of managing a wide range of tasks.

Another factor that was instrumental in shaping Gaskell's perspectives on herself and on her work was her affiliation with Unitarianism. Indeed, Gérin asserts that, outside the family orbit, the strongest single influence on her childhood was the religious training that she received in the Unitarian Chapel on Brook Street.[36] In Unitarian sermons and devotional literature, the word "culture" or "cultivation" is used repeatedly. According to Unitarian thought, a person is responsible for cultivating his or her own soul.[37] Indeed, Unitarianism emphasized the almost limitless capacity of human nature. This emphasis on human potential applied to women in a particularly significant way, affirming for them the possibility of self-knowledge and self-development.

Unitarianism freed Gaskell from some of the conventional and limiting views regarding women's proper activities. Lansbury notes that Unitarian women were normally educated in a manner comparable to men.[38] Further, she asserts that it was unusual for a Unitarian woman not to be informed about politics and science and not to be proficient in languages. The contrast between the tenets of domestic ideology and the tenets of Unitarianism is striking. Sarah Ellis urged women to suppress their own interests, to subordinate their talents, to work for others. Unitarianism, however, recommended cultivation of one's own gifts as a prerequisite to discovering one's own work. The Unitarian was obliged to pursue his or her own personal truth, and to act out that truth as an active member of society. If a woman discerned writing to be her talent, she viewed it not only as a gift, but a solemn duty as well, sent by God to be put to social use. Therefore, the woman writer had divine—if not always human—sanction for her work. Such a frame of mind contributed to a woman's sense that her life was not predetermined, that she was responsible for giving it meaning. Work was regarded as a form of self-definition and thus highly valued by the Unitarian.

One of Gaskell's letters contains an explicit statement about her view of work:

> I do believe we have all some appointed work to do, which no one else can do so well; Which is our work; what we have to do in advancing the Kingdom of God; and that first we must find out what we are sent into the world to do, and define it and make it clear to ourselves, (that's the hard part) and then forget ourselves in our work. (Letter 68)

On this issue Gaskell proved herself at odds with the Victorian association of true femininity with leisure. Because middle-class families measured wealth by the leisure afforded women, the definition of a lady depended upon her exemption from labor.[39] Victorian culture linked womanliness with inactivity. In contrast, Gaskell recognized not only women's potential for labor, but also their need for it.

Reading Elizabeth Gaskell in the 1990s is a startling experience because the writer once perceived as the quintessential Victorian lady can now be seen to confront problems familiar to contemporary women, problems that women are still attempting to solve. Successful at coordinating domestic duties and a career, Gaskell fits the image of the "Superwoman," a term used in the 1970s to denote a woman who could effortlessly merge her public and private roles. Gaskell managed simultaneously to attend to her responsibilities as a minister's wife, to bring up four daughters, and to secure a solid literary reputation for herself. Yet Gaskell's career was not without its efforts, strains, or costs. Throughout her life she was plagued with severe headaches, especially when she was under the pressure to write, and she died an early death at fifty-five, probably at the height of her powers. To a modern reader, her life appears to be symptomatic of the stresses of a time in which women's notions about vocation were beginning to change.

Gaskell sensed that she was living in a period of transition, and she looked to the future for the resolution of some of the issues and dilemmas confronting women. As she wrote novels that addressed the issue of work for women, she took a hopeful view of the possibilities that would be available to women in later years, while remaining aware of the present difficulties.

Unlike her contemporaries, Gaskell presents the process of finding one's vocation as central to a woman's life. While she does not eliminate courtship from the female narrative, neither does she offer it as the sole interest in a woman's life.[40] And, unlike Charlotte Brontë and George Eliot, Gaskell views women's labor as generally empowering and enriching. In chapter 2, I will examine several of Gaskell's contemporaries in order to contrast her treatment of women and work. In chapters 3-7, I discuss her five major works— *Mary*

Barton, North and South, Cranford, The Life of Charlotte Brontë, and *Wives and Daughters*—in order to demonstrate Gaskell's interest in the different directions that women take as they seek to find their work in the world. At the center of three of these works—*Mary Barton, North and South,* and *Wives and Daughters*—stands a bright, capable young woman whose life is all before her. What she makes of her life is the focus of each novel. In *Cranford,* Gaskell evokes the image of a female community that sustains itself by its own labor. In *The Life of Charlotte Brontë,* Gaskell is more constrained in her material, yet her goal is the same: to record and support the choices made by a woman as she pursued her life's work.

Gaskell's picture of a young factory girl, Mary Barton, who derives satisfaction as well as maturity from her occupation, is rare among Victorian images of working-class women. *Mary Barton* focuses on the career of a young, vital girl who is able to accomplish what she desires. Mary's father recognizes the importance of a vocation for his daughter and defers to her when she expresses an interest in becoming a seamstress. When Mary's mother dies, Mary, left to her own resources, becomes independent, making purchases on her own and conducting a romance with a young man of her own choosing. Mary's labor outside the home strengthens her to such an extent that she is able to execute a leading role in the public acquittal of her lover. At the end of the novel, Mary gets everything she wants—and she is confidently managing it all.

For other characters, factory work is not an appropriate option. Coming from a more genteel family background, Margaret Hale in *North and South* undergoes the process of defining her proper work, firmly rejecting the notion that idleness is fitting to a lady and coming to understand that she is responsible for her own life. A clergyman's daughter, Margaret moves with her father to industrial Lancashire, where her former comfortable life of privilege and freedom is replaced by the rigors of urban life in straitened circumstances. It is in such an atmosphere that Margaret grows in perception and power, willingly accepting the task of mediating between the agricultural South and the industrial North. Through her negotiations, the warring parties become reconciled and working conditions improve. *North and South* affirms women's right to participate in public life.

In *Cranford* Gaskell presents a community of women who are self-sufficient. These women have *chosen* to lead single lives and are happy in their choice. Although the inhabitants of Cranford are not wealthy, they do control property. In spite of their limited financial resources, the ladies of Cranford manage to create rituals and ceremonies that allow them to function comfortably, even on wafer bread and butter and sponge-biscuits. Furthermore, when disasters arise, they are able to find solutions and even to embark on new projects in old age. When the bank that serves Miss Matty fails, she faces the prospect of penury. Yet after a conference with her friends, she decides to support herself by selling tea, a scheme that flourishes due to the backing of her community. It is telling that Gaskell claimed this novel as her favorite, the one that gave her most pleasure: it is her most complete representation of a community of women who are content—and able—to pursue their own enterprises.

In *The Life of Charlotte Brontë*, Gaskell explores a figure in many ways like herself. A fellow woman and a fellow writer, Brontë embodies for Gaskell some of the complexities of her own situation. Gaskell knew how socially necessary it was for a woman writer to maintain a public image of womanliness while attempting to perform her work. As a result, she set for herself the task of reforming Brontë's image, or, as Carolyn Heilbrun puts it, of rescuing her from the "stigma of eccentricity."[41] Gaskell felt that Brontë's genius was well known; yet the public perception of her as deficient in traditionally feminine qualities was inaccurate. Gaskell wished therefore to reconcile the author's achievement with her femininity, thereby proving that the two could coexist. Admittedly, Gaskell does not concentrate on celebrating Brontë's genius, but that is not to say that she did not value it. Indeed, it was as an act of service to that genius that Gaskell attempted to rehabilitate her friend's reputation. Securing the image of the author would, Gaskell hoped, secure the work.

In *Wives and Daughters* Gaskell questions the limitations placed on young women through the character of Molly Gibson. Through Molly, Gaskell expresses her objection to her culture's prescription of idleness for its girls. Like Mary Barton, Molly Gibson is forced to grow up quickly in the absence of a mother. As a result she learns to be self-confident and self-determining. Molly develops a strong sense of personal identity, learning from both negative and positive female models. Like Mary Barton, Molly is unafraid to speak openly, even to challenge the authority of adults like her father. She is as capable intellectually as her future husband, Roger Hamley, participating in discussions with him about natural history; yet, because she is a young woman, she is denied the avenues for her talents that are available to him. Through Molly, Gaskell is criticizing a society that withholds from women opportunities for fulfilling work. Throughout her career Gaskell attempted to redefine femininity by associating it with the performance of labor and autonomy.

Notes

1. See "Sentimental Power: *Uncle Tom's Cabin* and the Politics of Literary History," in *The New Feminist Criticism*, ed. Elaine Showalter, 83, 100.

2. Cecil, *Victorian Novelists*, 184. Uglow's comprehensive new critical biography of Gaskell is a hopeful sign that Gaskell is beginning to be accorded a more important position in literary history.

3. See Ganz, *Elizabeth Gaskell*; Showalter, *A Literature of Their Own*; and Newton, *Women, Power, and Subversion*. Lovell, *Consuming Fiction*, observes that, among her contemporaries, Gaskell has received the least attention from feminist critics. Davis has rightly noted that Gaskell has "often bewildered feminist critics who do not find in her work the kind of protest that makes Bronte and George Eliot seem such modern women" ("Feminist Critics and Literary Mothers, 507).

Davis cites Gilbert and Gubar's omission of Gaskell as "striking evidence of feminist criticism's inability to incorporate Elizabeth Gaskell into the story it tells about women, submission, and resistance" (515). A recent critic, Felicia Bonaparte, argues that Gaskell is unaware of her own subversive "daemonic self" and remains throughout her life victimized by childhood traumas (*The Gypsy-Bachelor of Manchester*, 7, 56). Bonaparte's view of Gaskell is reminiscent of the view that many critics take of Charles Dickens, whom they see as eternally damaged by his childhood experiences. I regard Gaskell as far more canny and deliberate in her rebellion than does Bonaparte. The most recent exception to this general neglect and devaluation of Gaskell is Hilary Schor's compelling *Scheherezade in the Marketplace*. Schor places Gaskell within a feminist tradition, arguing that her experiments with literary form "led her to examine the central stories of her culture, particularly the conception of woman as the (silent) other" (5). Schor examines the "specific struggle of the woman writer with the literary plots she has inherited" and the "ways in which Scheherezade may have had to reimagine her own story" (4).

4. Macaulay, *Southey's Colloquies on Society*, 132.

5. Poovey, *Uneven Developments*, 3.

6. Carlyle, *Past and Present*, IV, 153.

7. Ibid., *Past and Present*, XII, 201-2.

8. Ibid., *Past and Present*, XI, 197.

9. For a useful overview of how cultural attitudes toward labor manifested themselves in literature see Rodgers, *The Work Ethic in Industrial America, 1850-1920*.

10. Carlyle, *Past and Present*, IV, 153.

11. Ibid., *Past and Present*, XII, 205.

12. This failure to acknowledge women's presence in the workforce seems to have been commonplace in America as well as in England. For an interesting analysis of the invisibility of women's work in the fiction of Harriet Beecher Stowe and Nathaniel Hawthorne, see Brown, *Domestic Individualism*.

13. Alexander, *Women's Work in Nineteenth Century London*, 36-7.

14. Gallagher persuasively argues that the rhetoric that was used in this discussion of women's work was often conflicted and contradictory. When reformers in the 1840s began to argue for protective legislation for workers, they employed the language of social paternalism and the language of domestic ideology, often in the same speech, as they lamented the suffering of women and the neglect of families while simultaneously condemning the growing independence of women. In short, family life—and especially the role of mothers—was subject to both idealization and censure. See *The Industrial Reformation of English Fiction*.

15. Victorian culture was insistent in representing women's labor as unalienated, outside of the realm of a waged economy. Poovey uncovers fissures in this discourse over women's labor in periodical literature, which admitted in articles about home management that work in the domestic sphere "might be as trying, in its own way, as work for money" (*Uneven Developments*, 157).

16. Green, *The Courtship Novel, 1740-1820*, has found in the novels of some two dozen writers evidence of a subgenre, termed by Green the "courtship novel," which considers the time between a young woman's coming out and her marriage as the most significant period of her life. The Victorians continued to evince enthusiasm for this period in a woman's life when she was considering and accepting the role her society recommended as her best possible course.

17. Poovey, *Uneven Developments*, 4.

18. Greg, "Why are Women Redundant," 436.

19. Ellis, *The Women of England*, 14.

20. Swindell, *Victorian Writing and Working Women*, 20.

21. Even Victorian feminists held many conventional notions about the nature of women. As Linda Hunt points out, Anna Jameson encouraged women to participate in the public sphere because she believed that their womanly qualities would transform the workplace. See *A Woman's Portion*, 6. Poovey also demonstrates that feminists like Barbara Bodichon and Jessie Boucherette often put their arguments about women's work in terms that their culture would accept. For example, one

argument they offered in support of women's entry into the workforce was the scarcity of husbands. See *Uneven Developments*, 158-9.

22. Ruskin, *Sesame and Lilies*, 59, 72, 62.

23. Ellis, *The Women of England*, 19.

24. Many of the works I describe are reproduced in Casteras' *Images of Victorian Womanhood in English Art*.

25. The opening line of *Jane Eyre* evokes the confined world the heroine must negotiate: "There was no possibility of taking a walk that day."

26. Brontë, *Jane Eyre*, 375, 393.

27. Brontë, *Villette*, 57, 92, 135.

28. Eliot, *Middlemarch*, 251, 575-6.

29. Du Plessis, *Writing beyond the Ending*, 3-4.

30. See *Relative Creatures*, 180. Although Hunt credits Charlotte Brontë's *Villette* with being the first English novel that treats the protagonist's work as "an integral part of her life," she also acknowledges Gaskell's contribution to this theme by calling her a "pioneer" who attempts "to expand the subject matter women writers dealt with" (*A Woman's Portion*, 83, 60).

31. On this important point, I am in disagreement with Calder, who contends that in Gaskell's fiction, women's work is linked with their imprisonment. See *Women and Marriage in Victorian Fiction*, 78.

32. Newton, *Women, Power, and Subversion*, 6, 7.

33. Gilligan's study demonstrates that ordinary women surveyed today still find themselves trying to balance how much they think they owe other people with how much they think they owe themselves. In the responses Gilligan has charted, female identity "is defined in a context of relationship and judged by a standard of responsibility and care." Gaskell wrestled with the same problem. See *In a Different Voice*, 160.

34. Levine, *Feminist Lives in Victorian England*, 46-7.

35. With wry wit, Brownstein draws a vivid picture of what life for Gaskell must have been like: "Consider Elizabeth Gaskell at her dining-room table, with her daughters and tradesmen and her husband's parishioners milling through, as she copes with one hand and, with the other, keeps stirring her novel" (*Becoming a Heroine*, 25).

36. Gérin, *Elizabeth Gaskell*, 13.

37. Robinson, *Apostle of Culture*, 10.

38. Lansbury, *Elizabeth Gaskell*, 4.

39. See Burstyn, *Victorian Education and the Ideal of Womanhood*, for a helpful account of the historical developments that led to the pressures on the middle-class woman *not* to work. Women's leisure became a measure of the economic success of men.

40. In fact, Beer claims that it was not until the end of her career, with the publication of *Wives and Daughters*, that Gaskell showed "thorough interest in the eternal who-marries-whom, which was the essential subject matter of so many previous novelists" (*Reader, I Married Him*, 155).

41. Heilbrun, *Writing a Woman's Life*, 22.

Chapter 2

The Industrial Novel:
Gaskell's Contemporaries

For some readers, the question of genre has been a key issue in placing Gaskell among other novelists of the nineteenth century. The centrality of social problems in Gaskell's fiction, particularly in *Mary Barton*, has been debated by the critics, who have expressed differing views of this aspect of her work. Wendy Craik has identified Gaskell as belonging to a group of writers whom she refers to as "provincial novelists." According to Craik, Dickens and Thackeray make London the norm, the "social and moral point of reference for the English novel."[1] In contrast, the provincial novelists, who include the then-popular but now-obscure Mary Russell Mitford as well as acknowledged greats like George Eliot, reject London as the center of their interests and instead locate their works in their own carefully chosen—often rural—settings. By selecting a different vantage point from which to view the world, these writers, Craik argues, are able to rise above social problems of the day and to write about unchanging, universal truths of the human condition. Craik also differentiates the provincial novelists from the novelists of social reform, like Disraeli and Kingsley, whose works are vehicles for social improvement. As Craik sees it, Elizabeth Gaskell's purpose in her novels is "to inform" rather than "to reform." And she asserts that Gaskell finally turns away from "vexed social questions" in her later novels. Other critics agree; according to Barbara Harman, Gaskell's exploration of social problems is "usually seen as marginal or subordinate to her 'real'—that is, personal—concerns."[2]

Margaret Ganz, on the other hand, sees Gaskell as the victim of warring impulses, including an impulse toward social reform, humor, commemoration, didacticism, melodrama, mystery, idyll, and tragedy.[3] Unlike Craik, Ganz believes that Gaskell falls short of being a great artist because she is *not* able to achieve the universality necessary for great literature. Although Craik and Ganz disagree on Gaskell's ultimate achievements in fiction, they nevertheless share a critical view that assumes that the messy texture of social life must be transcended and that the truly great will resist the temptation to inquire too deeply into contemporary problems.

Some recent critics have been more interested in the "social problem" side of Gaskell's fiction than of her so-called provincial or domestic realism side.[4] I would argue that there is no necessary conflict between "warring impulses" in Gaskell: whether she is writing humor, or writing a biography, or writing a novel of manners, she is above all, or, more accurately, underneath it all, writing about social problems—specifically identifying the problems within Victorian culture that are faced by its women. As feminists have long insisted, the "personal"—what goes on at home, in the domestic sphere—is political. We can find the same recognition in the works of Elizabeth Gaskell.

From the very beginning of her career, when she explores the industrial novel, Gaskell foregrounds the world of labor, bringing new concerns into the world of the novel. Moreover, throughout her entire career, she makes a plea for change, especially in the way that her culture views women. If one goes looking for a unifying thread throughout Gaskell's body of works, this one emerges insistently from beginning to end. However, protest is an inflammatory thing, especially for a woman writer. Gaskell's primary intention as an author is not to shock or to alienate her audience, but to persuade them. Therefore, to get her words out, Gaskell chooses to *displace* her feminist criticisms and assertions, as she experiments with several literary genres. The first is the congenial form of the industrial novel. For a Victorian writer who wished to explore social problems, this genre offered perhaps the most direct means of getting out a social message.

The industrial novel, described over thirty years ago by Kathleen Tillotson and Raymond Williams and redefined recently by Catherine Gallagher, is a genre that began to appear in the "hungry forties."[5] The term has been applied to a group of novels that includes *Sybil* (1845), *Mary Barton* (1848), *Alton Locke* (1850), *North and South* (1854), *Hard Times* (1854), and *Felix Holt* (1866). The industrial novels all share some common characteristics: the detailed documentation of the suffering of the poor, the reproduction of working-class speech through dialect, criticism of the effects of industrialism, the discussion of contemporary reform movements like Chartism and Utilitarianism, and some attempt—usually individual and internal—at a solution to social problems. Frequently the plot is developed around a sensitive protagonist, usually male, whose moral, intellectual, or emotional development spans the course of the novel and whose romantic attachments are troubled and conflicted. The protagonist is typically searching for a way to express or mitigate the dissatisfaction of the working class as he takes his role as their spokesman. The industrial novel, which combined narrative interest with protest, was a response to a particularly dismal period in which bank failures and the scarcity of jobs created conditions that many writers saw as deplorable. Dickens' choice of a title for his industrial novel, *Hard Times*, points to a common phrase workers used to describe a time when it was difficult to find adequate food and employment.

As machinery became more accessible and more complex, a large industrial working class formed. And as Britain took its place as a leading industrial nation, issues such as the employer's responsibility toward workers, working conditions, and wages began to be addressed in a variety of ways. The Parliamentary Commissions of Investigation represented the official governmental stance on the evolving social scene; the essays and novels written in the 1840s and 1850s were different kinds of attempts to explore contemporary problems and to suggest possible resolutions. Deirdre David has commented on the intimate connection between fiction of the period and the social facts that it addresses by asserting that the industrial novel is not outside the dilemmas that it examines, that the sometimes unbelievable endings of the industrial novels, with their reliance on coincidence and their easy reconciliation of class hostilities, are evidence that the novel is an "inseparable element, or symptom, of those same problems with which it explicitly sets out to concern itself."[6] She goes on to suggest that by creating a "myth of class cooperation" the industrial novelist seeks to do something about the workers' alienation from their work. Many of the industrial novelists identify the worker as male and explore the process of a man's finding his vocation. Unlike the other industrial novelists, Elizabeth Gaskell is primarily interested in how women fit into the new structures of society and in how work fits into a woman's life. A brief survey of several industrial novels will illuminate Gaskell's distinctiveness as she experiments with the genre.

Like most of the male writers who worked within the genre, Disraeli puts a male character at the center of the plot in *Sybil* (1845).[7] The novel focuses on a young aristocrat, Charles Egremont, who, "brought up in the enjoyment of every comfort and every luxury that refinement could devise and wealth furnish," develops a social conscience.[8] "Popular at school, idolized at home, . . . and secured [with] a family seat in Parliament," Egremont seems destined for a life of ease, until an unhappy love affair sends him abroad and he returns a "much wiser man" prepared "to observe, to inquire, and to reflect" (40). When female characters enter the plot in an industrial novel, they play conventional roles, serving mostly as romantic interests for the male protagonists. Sybil Gerard, the daughter of a factory worker of noble ancestry, serves as a difficult prize for Egremont to pursue and win in the course of the novel as well as a means of his introduction to the struggles of the working class. For a long while, Sybil's sense of the oppression of her people makes her inaccessible to Egremont, a member of the privileged class. Gradually Sybil's conviction that "to be one of the people was to be miserable and innocent; one of the privileged, a luxurious tyrant" is replaced by the realization that "the world was a more complicated system than she had preconceived" (337). In the end Sybil's aristocratic ancestry is revealed, and the conflict removed; Egremont and Sybil are free to marry.

Disraeli's portrayal of Sybil Gerard is an important issue in the novel, for it demonstrates the author's tendency to idealize women and to present them as uninvolved in the daily business of the world. From the beginning his characterization of Sybil establishes her as a spiritual creature who lives in a rarefied atmosphere where she is removed from the soil and toil of her supposed class. Thom Braun has suggested that Sybil's epithet, "The Religious," adequately expresses her role in the novel.[9] Egremont's first glimpse of Sybil reveals an otherworldliness that sets her apart from the rest of humanity:

> The divine melody ceased; the elder stranger rose; the words were on the lips of Egremont, that would have asked some explanation of this sweet and holy mystery, when, in the vacant and star-lit arch on which his glance was fixed, he beheld a female form. She was apparently in the habit of a Religious, yet scarcely could be a nun, for her veil, if indeed it were a veil, had fallen on her shoulders, and revealed her thick tresses of long fair hair. The blush of deep emotion lingered on a countenance which, though extremely young, was impressed with a character of almost divine majesty; while her dark eyes and long dark lashes, contrasting with the brightness of her complexion and the luxuriance of her radiant locks, combined to produce a beauty as rare as it is choice; and so strange, that Egremont might for a moment have been pardoned for believing her a seraph, who had lighted on this sphere, or the fair phantom of some saint haunting the sacred ruins of her desecrated fame. (77-78)

Sybil's ethereal qualities prevent her from developing a realistic, sophisticated view of the current political scene; instead, she takes a nostalgic view of the past, glorying in "a race of forefathers who belonged to the oppressed and not to the oppressors," and retreats to a dream world of her own making, envisioning a glorious future in which, through divine intervention, she and her father will regain their former landed status (291). So preoccupied is Sybil with this topic that, during a conversation with Egremont about the conditions of the working class, she remarks that the degradation of her faith and of her race are the only two topics that occupy her thoughts. Yet she does nothing at all to effect actual social change, believing that "nothing short of the descent of angels can save the people of this kingdom" (201). In contrast to the male view in the novel, expressed by Stephen Morley as "God will help those who help themselves," Sybil holds that "those only can help themselves whom God helps" (201). Unacquainted with the dynamics of actual political processes, Sybil is shocked to learn that the working class is deeply divided by internal factions, rivalries, intrigues. Although she is the daughter of a chief spokesman of the people, Sybil is naive in her political opinions and reveals only a tenuous grasp of what is taking place all around her.

This essentially passive view of human history is repeated in Sybil's response to the crises she is faced with in her own life. Despite her attraction to

Egremont, she rejects his offer of marriage, insisting that "a union between the child and brother of nobles and a daughter of the people" is impossible, that "the gulf is impassable" between them (324-5). Rather than attempting to find a solution to her personal dilemma, Sybil lets her abstract principles govern her, even when they will consign her to a life of self-denial.

Disraeli also denigrates his female character by presenting her as a powerless victim of circumstance. Sybil's greatest test comes when she learns that her father is in danger of being incarcerated and when she decides to try to reach him before the authorities do. In this moment of crisis, Disraeli emphasizes Sybil's feminine ineptitude, describing her at this moment, saying, "This child of innocence and divine thoughts, born in a cottage and bred in a cloister, went forth, on a great enterprise of duty and devotion, into the busiest and the wildest haunts of the greatest of modern cities" (359). The image he creates here is not one of a capable, decisive woman who takes matters into her own hands, but rather one of a young child who is protected by her very youth and vulnerability from injury. Throughout the scene Disraeli constantly emphasizes Sybil's weakness, mentioning her "sense of her utter helplessness," her "feminine reserve," her feeling of being "overpowered" (361). How she *feels*, not what she *does*, is Disraeli's focus. And when she does act, it is most often to implore for help. In the coffee house, the first words she speaks are "Is there not one among you who will assist me?" (361). When human help is not forthcoming, she seeks divine assistance, praying, "Holy Virgin, aid me!" (368). Finally encountering a kindly Irishman, she exclaims, "I beseech you by everything we hold sacred to aid me" (368). Later, she continues, "Guide me, I beseech you, honestly and truly guide me!" (368).

Moreover, despite her good intentions, Sybil cannot rescue her father; in the end it is she who needs to be rescued. "Pale, agitated, exhausted," arriving too late to save her father, Sybil is only able to whisper her warning and to look dumbly around her: "She looked up to her father, a glance as it were of devotion and despair; her lips moved, but they refused their office, and expressed no words" (379). Sybil actually makes the situation worse since her presence complicates matters for her father; after she faints she must be carried, a dead weight, in her father's arms. Ineffectual and inarticulate in an emergency, Sybil languishes until she thinks of a last resource, Egremont, and writes a letter to him, begging "Save me!" (384). Shrinking "with all the delicacy of a woman, from the impending examination in open court before the magistrate," Sybil is finally rescued by the intervention of the man who loves her and is again carried to her destination (386).

Throughout the novel Disraeli repeatedly shows Egremont coming to Sybil's rescue. When a mob of workers enters Mowbray Castle, Sybil makes an effort to repel them, but to little avail. Making a personal appeal, she attempts to shame the men into better behavior, chiding, "What is this? Are you led away by strangers to such deeds? Why, I know you all! You came here to aid, I am

sure, and not to harm" (477). Yet Sybil's hold on the crowd is short-lived, and
when she finds herself among strangers she is terrified for her safety as she
crouches in a corner of the flower garden. When a drunken ruffian grasps the
arm of Sybil, "an officer, covered with dust and gore, sabre in hand, jumped
from the terrace, and hurried to the rescue" (486).

Sybil's work in the novel is to allow herself to be instructed, assisted, won.
In contrast, Egremont's work is to discover his place in the political order and
to act within that order. His recognition that a life of ease and privilege is not
sufficient comes after a period of travel that helps him become "conscious he
wanted an object" (41). He begins "musing over action, though as yet ignorant
how to act" (41). This process of discerning his proper work in the world is
associated with his masculinity. As he gets closer to a sense of his own
vocation, Egremont "could not resist the conviction that . . . his sympathies had
become more lively and more extended; that a masculine impulse had been given
to his mind" (154). This masculine impulse spurs him to ask questions about
social conditions ("Why was England not the same land as in the days of his
light-hearted youth? Why were these hard times for the poor?") and to try to
determine the solution to the inequities that he sees (69). Gradually Egremont
comes to see himself as an orator who speaks for the interests of the people,
and, despite political risk, makes speeches in which he asserts that "the rights
of labour were as sacred as those of property; . . . that the social happiness of
the millions should be the first object of a statesman" (339). Unlike Sybil, a
"dreamer of dreams," Egremont is a man of action, taking his place in an
important national debate in the House of Commons. This discussion of the
National Petition is so weighty that "not a member was absent from his place;
men were brought indeed from distant capitals to participate in the struggle and
to decide it" (330). Disraeli's language is clear: politics is the work of men;
romance, the work of women.

Charles Kingsley's *Alton Locke* (1850) repeats many of the patterns found in
Disraeli, including an intellectual male protagonist who gradually comes to
recognize his work in the world.[10]   Kingsley's presentation of women,
however, is even less flattering than Disraeli's, for the biggest obstacle that
stands between Alton Locke and the development of his talents is his mother.
The one female character who is endowed with brains is inclined to throw her
energies into supporting Alton Locke, and not into developing them for herself.

The narrator, Alton Locke, is born into a social position and a family that
stifle his gifts and his imaginative nature. The opening sentences of the novel
suggest the dispiriting environment into which he is born: "I am a Cockney
among Cockneys. Italy and the Tropics, the Highlands and Devonshire, I know
only in dreams. Even the Surrey Hills, of whose loveliness I have heard so
much, are to me a distant fairyland."[11] Just as his knowledge of England is
"bounded by the horizon which enriches Richmond Hill," so his interests, plans,
dreams are bounded by the circumstances in which he finds himself (1). The

picture Kingsley paints from the start is one of confinement.

The primary obstacle to Alton's intellectual and artistic development is his mother, who moves "by rule and method" (3). A strict Calvinist, his mother is reluctant to exhibit affection for her children, believing that such displays are "carnal." Worse than her distant manner, her assumption that her son is not one of the elect causes her to punish and dismiss him when he formulates questions and expresses doubts about her oppressive brand of religion. Discouraged from thinking independently, Alton must hide his creative productions, as he does a little poem he has written about God's love for one and all.

In his presentation of the mother, Kingsley suggests that women can be dangerous because they stand between a man and his work. Alton's apprenticeship as a tailor begins the process of separation from his dominating mother, a process that is never fully complete, for, long after her death, her image haunts and judges him. With her approval, Alton is sent to a workshop and is immediately repulsed by the dirt, cold, and human wreckage he finds there. Throughout the novel Kingsley presents work as dispiriting, setting the "soulless routine of mechanical labour," "the hell of mere manual drudgery," against the possibility of creative and spiritual fulfillment (64, 63). Unable to confide in his mother about the conditions he has met with in the workshop, Alton assumes that she knows what the place is like and believes it appropriate for him. From that point, Alton says, "a gulf was opening between us; we were moving in two different worlds, and she saw it, and imputed it to me as a sin" (20).

Alton's first overt act of disobedience is to select his own reading material, something that his mother has forbidden. Because he is forced to conceal his efforts at self-improvement from her, he wakes at two in the morning to read by candlelight. Finally discovered at his Virgil, Alton must face the constant scrutiny of his mother, who becomes suspicious of all his comings and goings. An argument over religion finally prompts her to say, "Leave this house this moment. You are no son of mine henceforward" (42).

In his presentation of Alton and his mother, Kingsley pits intellect against irrationality, curiosity against dogma. The first woman in Alton's life proves to be not only unsupportive but also harmful to his spiritual development. His mother leaves such a painful legacy that for many years Alton rejects Christianity altogether. Kingsley's depiction of Alton's sister is very similar, for, although he has fond memories of their childhood moments together—as he has pleasant memories of his mother—he becomes estranged from his sister after she becomes a copy of their mother. These unflattering portrayals point to an underlying conclusion: that men with a special mission often have to reject women since they can hinder a man in the achievement of his work.

In his delineation of Lillian, "beautiful, beautiful, beyond all statue, picture, or poet's dream," Kingsley makes much the same point (54). After seeing Lillian briefly in an art gallery, Alton is haunted for years by the image of her lovely face and neglects his own education and his own health in his persistent efforts to find her again. Furthermore he expends his energies in jealousy as he engages in a rivalry with his ambitious cousin, who finally wins Lillian's hand in marriage. Although Lillian is well read and cultivated, she lacks commitment and purpose. Kingsley makes it clear that she takes only a casual interest in Alton as a specimen of the working class. A distraction from his work, Lillian is finally exposed as unworthy of his devotion. Kingsley's treatment of both Alton's mother and Lillian implies that women are impediments to the work of men.

Lillian's cousin, Eleanor Staunton, is the novel's one example of the intellectual and spiritual woman. With a beauty "rather of a Juno than a Venus—dark, imperious, restless— . . . rather to be feared than loved," Miss Staunton is overshadowed by the more conventionally pretty Lillian (115). Perceived by Alton as "harsh," Miss Staunton is not afraid to challenge the ideas and assertions of men. Alton complains that her manner to him was "dictatorial and abrupt" and that she "made a point of carping at chance words of mine, and of setting me down, suddenly, by breaking in with some severe, pithy observation, on conversations to which she had been listening unobserved" (132). The dean takes Miss Staunton seriously enough to engage in debate with her, and Alton's cousin acknowledges "she is uncommonly well read; and says confounded clever things, too" (134).

Eleanor Staunton proves herself to be an intellectual match for Alton Locke. And, in the course of the novel, she proves to be his spiritual superior. However, Miss Staunton remains in the background, intervening only when Alton needs help and choosing to be a secret benefactor until the very end of the novel. Because the novel charts the development of Alton, Miss Staunton must be kept in the background; interesting and complex though she is, she cannot take center stage.

In Alton Locke and Eleanor Staunton, Kingsley draws competing characters. Kingsley includes details about the careers of both Alton Locke and Eleanor Staunton but focuses on Alton, the weaker character. Throughout much of the novel, Alton acts in undecidedly unheroic fashion, making mistakes and repeatedly compromising his principles. When his employer announces that the tailors' workrooms are to be closed and the system of home work instituted, Alton joins with his co-workers in a protest against such an exploitative change in labor arrangements. Initially this looks like a triumph of the individual over oppression. Yet almost immediately the actual consequences of Alton's action become clear: because he is out of work, he is forced to become a hack writer in order to support himself. In effect, he trades one form of compromise for another, putting "Pegasus into heavy harness" (147). In the same way, Alton agrees to let the controversial passages from his poems be cut out "for the sake of popularity, money, patronage," inspiring a reprimand "Weak!" from Miss Staunton (142).

Alton's worst moment comes when he attempts to conduct a Chartist meeting in a rural area and the meeting turns into a riot. Stung by the ridicule of his friends, Alton volunteers to lead the deputation and to offer the support of the London chapter. Once there, after a series of bitter speeches by starving laborers, Alton stands up and assures them of the sympathy of the London working men and asks for their assistance in obtaining parliamentary representation. Inexperienced before a crowd, Alton does not know how to answer their surly replies "that they did not know anything about politics—that what they wanted was bread" (210). All of his abstract arguments fail with his audience, who continue to shout for bread. Finally, desperate, he agrees with them, telling the crowd to go and get bread. Chaotic and violent acts follow, acts that Alton is powerless to stop. Later Alton must face a prison term for his participation in this sequence of events.

As a result of his experiences—as a poor tailor struggling to improve himself and as a Chartist struggling to improve the lot of the working class—Alton Locke comes to value deeds over action, practice over theory. When he is in prison, Alton is ministered to by a clergyman whose opinions differ from his own. At the same time, Alton recognizes the genuinely charitable behavior of the clergyman, saying, "While such thy deeds, what matter thine opinions?" (226). But judged by his own standard, Alton does not fare well. Tempted by the promise of recognition, offended by the criticism of others, ineffectual in the face of crises, Alton does not seem like much of a hero.

In contrast, Eleanor Staunton possesses all the qualities of a hero, but Kingsley will not let her be one. After her marriage to Lord Ellerton, changes in the management of his estate begin to occur; these changes include the construction of schools and churches, the improvement of cottages, the establishment of communal living arrangements, and the introduction of books and art into the lives of the laborers. Behind many of these changes stands Lady Staunton, "aiding, encouraging, originating . . . in all these noble plans" (184). After her husband's death, she chooses to live with the needlewomen for a year, spending her fortune on the poor and supporting herself without the help of a servant "to see what it was really like" (277). As a result of that experience, she organizes a large house for fifty women to live in together as they work and share the earnings among themselves. Lady Staunton has a radical social vision and works to realize it:

> I tried association among my own sex—among the most miserable and degraded of them. I simply tried to put them into a position in which they might work for each other, and not for a single tyrant . . . . Experienced men warned me that I should fail; that such a plan . . . demanded what was impossible to find, good faith, fraternal love, overruling moral influence. I answered, that I knew that already; that nothing but Christianity alone could supply that want, but that it could and should supply it; that I would teach them to live as sisters, by living with them as their sister myself. (296)

Despite her considerable gifts and her considerable accomplishments, Eleanor Staunton regards her chief work in life as supporting the work of a man. After she shares with Alton her Christian vision of social reorganization, she confesses to him that the highest of all her hopes was "that God would allow me, ere I die, to save a man . . . , a man of the people, whom I could train to be the poet of the people" (302). Her last charge to Alton Locke is that he should "publish, in good time, an honest history" of his life (305). And so we have the novel. Kingsley could not imagine—and therefore could not write—an account of a woman's journey toward her own life's work.

Both Dickens and Eliot devote more attention to a female character than does either Disraeli or Kingsley. But in *Hard Times* (1854) Dickens' characterization of the passive, easily victimized Louisa Gradgrind contrasts sharply with Gaskell's characterization of strong, self-reliant women in her novels. Along with her siblings, Louisa is indoctrinated from childhood into the rigid system of her father, "a man of fact and calculations," whose credo is "You are to be in all things regulated and governed . . . by fact."[12] "Lectured at . . . coursed, like little hares," his children are manipulated and controlled until they are almost beyond hope of achieving any personal identity. Once Louisa reaches adolescence, she tries to seek out alternative realms of experience, going secretly to the circus because she "wanted to see what it was like" (57). Dissatisfied with the narrow boundaries that surround her life, Louisa possesses an "air of jaded sullenness" (57). Dickens likens her to "a light with nothing to rest upon, a fire with nothing to burn, a starved imagination keeping life in itself somehow" (57). Deprived of any play for what Dickens calls "fancy," Louisa is presented as doomed to be a victim of her circumstances.

Although Louisa is not literally motherless, as so many of Gaskell's heroines are, she is nevertheless lacking in motherly guidance. Mrs. Gradgrind, befuddled from all of the stern teaching her husband insists on, dismisses her children with the injunction "Go and be somethingological directly" (61). Abdicating her maternal role, Mrs. Gradgrind abandons the restless Louisa, making her vulnerable to the matrimonial designs of Mr. Bounderby. While Dickens is careful to show that young Tom is also victimized by his upbringing, he consistently emphasizes Louisa's sexual defenselessness. Aware that Mr. Bounderby is interested in her, yet ignorant of how to discourage or refuse him, Louisa simply endures his attentions. Louisa realizes her own deficiency but is unable to correct it; as she tells her brother, "I don't know what other girls know" (91). Tom at least has the chance to escape from an oppressive home environment when he takes a position at Bounderby's office; Louisa, in contrast, has nothing to look forward to. Gazing into the fire, she confides to her mother, makes her think "how short my life would be, and how little I could hope to do in it" (94). Dickens juxtaposes Tom's confidence that he will be able to "manage and smoothe old Bounderby" with Louisa's profound sense of futility and purposelessness (92).

In his depiction of Louisa, Dickens implies that intellect is a harmful burden for a woman and that her natural realm is the realm of feeling. Louisa's lack of emotional development alienates her from others and from herself. In a comment to the circus child, Sissy Jupe, Louisa reveals her feeling of perpetual estrangement: "You are more useful to my mother, and more pleasant with her than I can ever be . . . . You are pleasanter to yourself, than I am to myself" (96). The strongest attachment Louisa feels is to her brother, and it is her brother's wish that she accept Mr. Bounderby that decides Louisa's response to his marriage proposal. Alienated from the emotional resonance of such a decision, Louisa considers her marriage from a purely practical point of view, reasoning that, since life is short, "while it lasts, I would wish to do the little I can, and the little I am fit for. What does it matter!" (136).

Like Gaskell's Margaret Hale in *North and South*, Louisa is forced to confront the class divisions between the hands and the masters when her attention is drawn to the plight of an individual worker. Yet she is far less successful than Gaskell's character in addressing a painful situation. After Stephen Blackpool is discharged by her husband, Louisa makes a visit to his home and tries to offer him money. The meeting is something of a revelation to her, but she is unable to be of much help to the man she pities. Moreover, she is the unwitting cause of his betrayal, for, by bringing her brother into the situation, she makes it possible for Tom to set up a scene that will ultimately ruin Blackpool's reputation. Dickens clearly presents Louisa as well-intentioned, yet he also makes it clear that innocence can have disastrous effects. Ineffectual in bringing about class reconciliation, Louisa actually contributes to the destruction of one worker.

Inexperienced with romance, Louisa is also ill-equipped to handle the sophisticated James Harthouse, whose cynical stance that everything is a sham seems indistinguishable from her father's principles. Realizing that the way to get to Louisa is through her brother, Harthouse pretends to be concerned about Tom's gambling debts, as well as his ungracious treatment of his generous sister. Louisa, unaware that she is being manipulated, begins to respond to Harthouse, who finally takes advantage of Bounderby's absence to declare himself her lover. Uncertain about her feelings, Louisa flees to her father, confessing her lack of moral underpinnings and utter dissatisfaction with her life and asking for some sort of guidance: "All that I know is, your philosophy and your teaching will not save me. Now, father, you have brought me to this. Save me by some other means!" (242)

Louisa gradually works her way out of this collapse with the help of another young woman, Sissy Jupe. The daughter of a circus clown, Sissy responds instinctively and sympathetically to the hardened, weary Louisa, bringing her radiant presence into the dark room where Louisa slowly recovers. Throughout the novel, Dickens associates Sissy with a warm, cheerful light; for example, when Louisa's sister, Jane, comes into the sickroom, Louisa observes, "What a beaming face you have, Jane!", prompting Jane to respond, "Have I? . . . I am sure it must be Sissy's doing" (243). Indeed, Sissy's presence in the house brings healing to all those whom Mr. Gradgrind's system had damaged. Even he is aware of the transformation, as he comments to his daughter, "Louisa, I have a misgiving that some change may have been slowly working about me in this house, by mere love and gratitude; that what the Head had left undone and could not do, the Heart may have been doing silently" (246). Here Dickens is drawing on a tenet of Victorian domestic ideology that associates women with feeling, femininity with the heart. For Louisa to become whole, she must replace the training of the intellect with the training of the heart.

Like Molly Gibson in *Wives and Daughters*, Sissy is not afraid to act as an advocate for her compromised friend. Taking it upon herself to expel Harthouse, Sissy confronts the worldly man, armed with nothing but "child-like ingenuousness," "modest fearlessness," "truthfulness which put all artifice aside" (253). And, like Margaret Hale in *North and South*, Sissy relies on her very vulnerability as a woman to keep her free from injury. However, unlike Dickens, Gaskell is aware that women do not live charmed lives: Margaret is injured when she tries to shield John Thornton from an angry crowd of workers, and Molly Gibson's reputation is soiled when people assume that she is conducting a romance with John Preston when she is in reality trying to help her friend get out of one. Dickens does what Gaskell will not do for her characters: he puts a protective shield around Sissy so that she goes completely unscathed from her meeting with Harthouse and in fact triumphs completely over the disconcerted cynic, sending him out of town and out of Louisa's life forever. Dickens suffuses Sissy with symbolic light, making her a kind of bright angel who helps Louisa begin life anew.

The best that Dickens can do for Louisa is to introduce her to family scenes, indicating that the most satisfying place for a woman is beside the domestic hearth.[13] To the end a victim of her early environment, Louisa must go backwards and start anew; it is necessary for her to grow "learned in childish lore" and to surround herself with children—Sissy's children, not her own (313). Her work in the course of the novel is to become a little child again; Dickens will not even allow her the conventional novelistic reward for women: marriage and children of her own.

In *Felix Holt* (1866) George Eliot comes closest to making a female character the center of her novel in her portrait of the daughter of a dissenting minister, Esther Lyon.[14] Eliot is interested in tracing the spiritual journey of a young woman whose understanding is deepened when she is exposed to attitudes and values that are very different from her own. Like many of Gaskell's characters, Esther is intellectually lively, yet unlike Gaskell's characters, at the beginning she is morally immature. With her refined tastes, she delights most in her own creature comforts, spending her wages on wax (not tallow) candles, attar of rose, collections of Byron's poetry. Through her relationship to a young radical, Felix Holt, Esther becomes aware of the possibility of a nobler life, one that is not founded upon the satisfaction of purely personal desires, but dedicated to an idea, a hope that the condition of the working class can be improved.

Esther Lyon must be made to see the inadequacy of her set of values; her work is to be receptive to a new set of political ideas. Unlike Gaskell, Eliot insists on the necessity of masculine guidance in this process of female development. While in *North and South* Margaret Hale is influenced by the ideas of her lover, there is at the same time an *exchange*: he, in turn, gradually accepts some of hers as well. In contrast, the proposal scene in *Felix Holt* concludes with a conversation in which Esther murmurs "with a grave look of appealing submission . . . 'I wish to do what you think it will be right to do.'"[15] Although Eliot accords more attention to female struggles, temptations, and needs than does Kingsley or Disraeli, she is as skeptical as they about the possibility of men and women teaching and learning from each other as they work together toward some goal in the world.

Throughout the novel Eliot represents the male and female spheres as separate and unbridgeable. The opening of the novel, with its inexorable focus on the dissatisfied Mrs. Transome, sketches out the arena of activity available to women—and its rigid boundaries. Because her husband is incapacitated by a paralytic seizure, Mrs. Transome had for a long time assumed many of the duties belonging to the master of the estate. When her son returns home, he determines to correct the situation, telling his mother, "Ah, you've had to worry yourself about things that don't properly belong to a woman . . . . We'll set all that right" (21). Accustomed to being "chief bailiff, and to sit[ting] in the saddle two or three hours every day," Mrs. Transome wishes to continue to be "consulted on all things," but her son, who believes that women are "slight things," resolves to consign her to satin cushions, feeling certain of the "general futility of women's attempts to transact men's business" (18, 110). Mrs. Transome's sense of her own powerlessness, her recognition that "there's no pleasure for old women," stems in part from the possession of abilities and the lack of a socially acceptable way to express those same abilities (29). In this situation, Mrs. Transome represents for Eliot "a woman's hunger of the heart forever unsatisfied" (30). A little daily embroidery, that "soothing occupation of taking stitches," becomes Mrs. Transome's only resource (95). Like Gaskell, Eliot believes that maternity is not all-sufficient to occupy the minds of women, that "mothers have a self larger than their maternity" (114). But Eliot is more at a loss than Gaskell in pointing the way to a possible reconciliation between family and self-fulfillment.

In the same way that Mrs. Transome is fond of her freedom and her intellectual superiority, Esther Lyon prefers to follow her own pursuits and rejects those that society is willing to confer upon her. Working as a governess does not please Esther: "The position of servitude was irksome to her" (79). Faced with few options, Esther chooses to live at home with her father, where she is able to enjoy "comparative independence" (79). However, Esther's idea of independence is to be able to use up all of her earnings to buy the finest cambric handkerchiefs and the freshest gloves. Eliot is critical of Esther's shallowness and makes it clear that she thinks that Esther deserves the lectures Felix Holt directs at her. In fact, their courtship consists of a series of meetings in which Felix challenges and corrects Esther's choice of reading material, statements, perceptions. After reproaching her for having "enough understanding to make it wicked that [she] should add one more to the women who hinder men's lives from having any nobleness in them," Felix tells Esther directly that he wishes her to change (125). Although Esther at first "revolted against his assumption of superiority, yet she felt herself in a new kind of subjection to him" (129).

The process of improvement in Esther begins with self-examination and with acts of self-denial, such as noticing her father's needs and providing for them. The process also involves cultivating an interest in political activities, as when Esther decides to listen to speeches in the marketplace, an act that is not approved by the town's matrons. Most dramatic of all is Esther's participation in the trial of Felix Holt. Wrongly accused of leading a riot, Felix is also charged with murder; his vindication rests with the witnesses who will speak for him. When Esther realizes that she possesses information that might help clear Felix, she, a woman who has always been acutely aware of the image she presents to the world, steps forward to present evidence on her lover's behalf. Eliot writes, "There was no blush on her face: she stood divested of all personal considerations, whether of vanity or shyness" (448). Eliot praises Esther's "inspired ignorance," her "reverence" for the man who stood unjustly accused (447). And Eliot emphasizes the tremendous effort that it was for Esther to speak: "The acting out of that strong impulse had exhausted her energy" (449). Unlike Mary Barton, Esther does not have an immediate or significant effect on the outcome of the trial; unlike Gaskell, who allows a woman's acts to have a real effect on the course of events, Eliot presents her character's act as a personal victory over self-absorption; it takes subsequent intervention by men to free Holt.

While Esther is required to change in the course of the novel, Felix remains essentially the same. Resolved from the beginning that a career as a radical would preclude his marriage, Felix states plainly his intentions to remain single. Although he finds himself attracted to Esther, "he was not going to let her have any influence on his life" (231). Esther believes that "she could never be good without him," but Felix is convinced that he can be good only without her (312). Driven by his sense of his own particular calling to live among the poor and to try to make their lot better, Felix finally consents to marry a chastened and submissive Esther. Her work is to become marriageable, to become fit not to hinder his. Through Esther, Eliot suggests that "a woman . . . could not make her own lot," that she can only choose between possibilities that present themselves to her.   And, for Eliot, women's choices usually involve renunciation: Esther must give up the refined life that as an heiress she has a legitimate claim to and must instead meet the "summons to a daily task" and face "the dim life of the back street" (465).

As developed by Disraeli, Kingsley, Dickens, and Eliot, the industrial novel does not offer much to women. It assigns them only a limited role in the plot and denies them much of an effect on the chain of events. As we shall see in the next chapter, by using some of the plot conventions and stock scenes of the genre, Gaskell makes the industrial novel a form that affirms women's abilities and needs.

Notes

1. Craik, *Elizabeth Gaskell and the English Provincial Novel*, ix.

2. Harman, "In Promiscuous Company," 360.

3. Ganz, *Elizabeth Gaskell*.

4. See, for example, Bodenheimer, *The Politics of Story in Victorian Social Fiction*; Harman, "In Promiscuous Company: Female Public Appearance in Elizabeth Gaskell's *North and South*"; and David, *Fictions of Resolution in Three Victorian Novels*.

5. For landmark discussions of the industrial novel, see Tillotson, *Novels of the Eighteen Forties*; Williams, *Culture and Society, 1780-1950*; and Gallagher, *The Industrial Reformation of English Fiction*.

6. David, *Fictions of Resolution in Three Victorian Novels*, 7.

7. For a recent discussion of this little-known novel, see McCully, "Beyond 'The Convent and the Cottage.'"

8. Disraeli, *Sybil, or The Two Nations*, 33; hereafter, page numbers are cited in parentheses in the text.

9. Braun, *Disraeli the Novelist*, 105.

10. Yeazell points out, however, that Kingsley's poet-tailor is considerably more feminized than the heroes of other industrial novels, such as Felix Holt ("Why Political Novels Have Heroines").

11. Kingsley, *Alton Locke*, 1; hereafter, page numbers are cited in parentheses in the text.

12. Dickens, *Hard Times*, 48, 52; hereafter, page numbers are cited in parentheses in the text.

13. Gallagher argues that the ending of the novel is a retreat into the purely private sphere (*The Industrial Reformation of English Fiction*, 155).

14. For a recent discussion of this novel, see Rogers, "Lessons for Fine Ladies."

15. Eliot, *Felix Holt the Radical*, 474; hereafter, page numbers are cited in parentheses in the text.

Chapter 3

"The Hidden Power . . . in the Outward Appearance": *Mary Barton*

Like Disraeli's *Sybil*, Kingsley's *Alton Locke*, Dickens' *Hard Times*, and Eliot's *Felix Holt*, *Mary Barton* is an industrial novel that makes its contribution to the Condition of England question. Kathleen Tillotson has suggested that Gaskell differs from these other novelists in "having no axe to grind."[1] On the contrary, I believe that Gaskell does indeed have an axe to grind: in this novel and in subsequent novels, Gaskell focuses on the problems of women in nineteenth-century England. In *Mary Barton* Gaskell uses the industrial novel to criticize the dominant ideology that separates the sexes, to make a feminist statement about women's need for meaningful work, and to affirm their fitness for participation in the public sphere. In this novel, Gaskell challenges the Victorian conception of a gender-based division of labor that separated the public and private domains.

A woman writer with an axe to grind in Victorian England had to be very careful—and very clever. As a thirty-eight year-old minister's wife, Gaskell was certainly aware of the risks she was taking. Her reputation—and that of her husband, a well-known public man—was at stake. Her comments on her first novel demonstrate that the writing of this novel was for her a matter of great urgency and even anxiety, hence her choice to publish it anonymously. To Mary Ewart she displayed agitation at being identified as the author: "I did write it, but how did you find it out? I *do* want it to be concealed if possible, and I don't think anybody here has the least idea who is the author . . . . I am almost frightened at my own action in writing it" (Letter 36). She was frightened for good reason; despite the approval of many readers, the publication of the novel brought upon Gaskell attacks by individuals and critics who believed that she failed to represent in her novel the perspective of management.[2]

Gaskell's letters shed light on the thinking process that culminated in the novel. According to her own account, she had long felt that "the bewildered life of an ignorant, thoughtful man of strong power of sympathy, dwelling in a town so full of striking contrasts as this is, was a tragic poem" (Letter 39). This description of the novel's subject omits Mary Barton altogether. Interestingly, Gaskell originally intended to call the novel *John Barton*, until her publisher hit upon the final title of the work.[3] Coral Lansbury notes that in writing *Mary Barton* Gaskell followed the same pattern that she followed in the composition of all her novels, eventually turning her attention to a female character: "Although its original conception may have been the story of a man . . . it became, in the course of development, the story of a young woman."[4] Either Gaskell did not initially plan for the young woman to take center stage in the novel, or, equally likely, by creating the impression that she would focus on a male character, she was "selling" the novel in terms she thought the reading public would buy; the real subject had to remain covert. That Gaskell accepted the proposed change suggests that she recognized the underlying implications of her material, and explains why she was a bit frightened at having written it.

The painful personal circumstances that led to the writing of *Mary Barton*—the loss of a much-loved child—were, by her own admission, the wellsprings of Gaskell's fiction. The death of her ten-month-old son of scarlet fever is frequently cited as the event that prompted Gaskell to write; the usual account is that William Gaskell, seeing his wife paralyzed with sorrow, suggested that she write to distract her mind, and thus we have *Mary Barton*. However, interestingly, Margaret Homans has discovered that twelve years earlier, in 1833, Gaskell had given birth to a stillborn daughter. This event was commemorated three years later by a sonnet that declares the mother's intention never to forget this daughter. This first literary effort was never published, an indication of how deeply the experience affected Gaskell.[5] Grief over a daughter lies underneath the narrative of *Mary Barton*. A writer—who is also a mother—attempts to assuage her own pain—and the pain of other women—by expressing it.

However, Gaskell is not solely preoccupied with her own pain. Her principal purpose is to depict the distance between the classes and the pressures under which working-class people lived. In particular, Gaskell is concerned with working women, the largest group in Victorian England whose labor was not fully recognized or sanctioned.[6] Drawing on the pain she felt during the loss of her own children, Gaskell attempts to express in *Mary Barton* the difficult situation faced by Victorian women within a culture that neither recognized nor rewarded their labor.

In *Mary Barton* Gaskell enters territory that is new. Françoise Basch asserts that Elizabeth Gaskell is the only one of the major writers of the first half of the Victorian era to have explored in some detail the subject of female labor.[7] She goes on to point out that although she treats the professions of governess and schoolteacher less fully than Charlotte Brontë, Gaskell exhibits more of an interest in jobs that are done by working women—nurses, dressmakers, factory workers—subject matter that was generally ignored in novels of the period.[8]

Gaskell was keenly aware that she was opening up an alien social territory to her readers. Although working-class participation in the reading audience has been documented, and the rise of the mechanics institutes attested to the interest in reading among members of the working class, regular reading was more typical of the middle class. Both skilled and unskilled laborers put in long hours; a fourteen-hour day was commonplace, and a sixteen-hour day not unusual. The most privileged workers came home no earlier than six or seven o'clock in the evening, a schedule that left little time and energy for reading. And since Saturday was often the busiest and longest workday, that left only Sunday for reading (witness the great popularity of the Sunday paper and the weekly miscellany that was issued on Saturday).[9] *Mary Barton* was published anonymously, as part of a series by Chapman and Hall, and came out in two volumes. The novel, Tillotson explains, was likely to have taken immediate buyers, for it was topical and, at eighteen shillings, affordable.[10] Clearly, *Mary Barton* would have drawn its readership mostly from the middle class.

Therefore, Gaskell must have known that most of her readers would have been unfamiliar with the lives led by common laborers. She acknowledges this early in the novel: "There is a class of men in Manchester, unknown even to many of the inhabitants, and whose existence will probably be doubted by many."[11] She goes on to describe manual laborers, weavers, who manipulate the shuttle while glancing at the open book on the loom, who take a genuine interest in mathematical problems or discussions of natural history. At the end of the passages, Gaskell writes, "Such are the tastes and pursuits of some of the thoughtful, little understood, working men of Manchester" (76). This passage could only have been written in response to the isolation between classes that was so troubling to the industrial novelists. To say that the very existence of a group will be doubted is to document the social stratification that Gaskell is attacking. Within this context, Gaskell's purpose is twofold: first, to introduce one class to another; second, to present the working class sympathetically.

In *Mary Barton*, Gaskell's focus is on working-class society, in which young women were freer from the conventions governing feminine behavior, since they lived outside the boundaries of gentility. One of the problems addressed by the novel is the separation between classes and genders; Gaskell wants her novel to bridge the boundaries between her characters and her readers and to discourage a middle-class sense of complacent superiority. The novel opens with a scene of working-class life, centering especially upon factory girls, to whom Gaskell attributes both energy and vitality: "Groups of merry and somewhat loud-talking girls, whose ages might range from twelve to twenty, came by with a buoyant step" (40). Although, the narrator says, "their faces were not remarkable for beauty," they possessed "an acuteness and intelligence of countenance" (41). When these young women were approached by groups of young men, they "held themselves aloof, not in a shy, but rather in an independent way" (41). From the start, Gaskell's intention is to emphasize the strength and vitality of working-class girls, characterizing them as active, bright, and self-sufficient.[12] By presenting working-class life positively, as fostering in women some qualities that would enrich and improve their lives, Gaskell is interested in dispelling the notion that work destroys femininity.

Central to this purpose is Gaskell's presentation of Mary, the main character of the novel. The reader's first glimpse of Mary reveals a young woman who is actively engaged, constantly *doing*.[13] At the same time, Gaskell makes a point of presenting her as attractive and successful when she carries out traditionally feminine duties. Mary first enters the novel as a "bonny lassie of thirteen or so" who "came bounding along to meet and to greet her father" (47). When an "over-grown lad" comes past her, stealing a kiss, "more with anger than shame . . . she slapped his face." When her father holds her infant brother out, she "sprang forward to take her father's charge." On the way home, two boys, seeing Mary walking with Jem Wilson, called out "Eh, look! Polly Barton's gotten a sweetheart," at which point Mary "assume[d] the air of a young fury, and to his next speech she answered not a word" (49). As a result, throughout the novel Mary is portrayed as *acting*; the reader's interest in her lies in what she *does*. No decorative fixture in the home, Mary moves freely in and out, exercising her own judgment as she goes about her daily activities.

In this novel Gaskell is responding to domestic ideology, which forbids activity and recommends decorous passivity or selfless servitude for women. Consequently, from the earliest chapters, she emphasizes affirmative images of women working. While John Barton and his friend, Wilson, are discussing the fate of Esther, Barton's sister-in-law, whose vanity and love of finery have led her, Barton suspects, into ruin, Barton declares that he'd rather see his daughter "earning her bread by the sweat of her brow, as the Bible tells her she should do . . . than be like a do-nothing lady, worrying shopmen all morning, and screeching at her pianny all afternoon, and going to bed without having done a good turn to any one of God's creatures but herself" (44). Wilson praises his sister, Alice, by noting her readiness to work: "Though she may have done a hard day's wash, there's not a child ill within the street but Alice goes to offer to sit up, and does sit up too, though may be she's to be at her work by six next morning" (46). Idleness is viewed as evidence of moral defectiveness; working, on the other hand, is a positive value because it produces human sympathy and creates community. The novel's depiction of women at their work indicates that Gaskell views activity—not inertia—as appropriate for young women.

Moreover, Gaskell represents working-class family life as enacting positive values of cooperation and shared work. Since working-class men and women share in the labor outside the home, they are, Gaskell suggests, more successful at creating equitable arrangements within it.[14] Common participation in the workforce—a public act—impinges on the private domain of the home. In contrast, middle-class society is based on the separation of the sexes; men become producers in the waged economy while women remain at home and function economically as consumers. In her depiction of the working-class households within the novel, Gaskell is recommending an alternative to the gendered organization of labor in the home.

Mary Barton demonstrates the benefits of men and women sharing the workload. While on an outing with their neighbors, John Barton motions his wife and her friend to the ground after spreading his handkerchief and says, "Now, Mrs. Wilson, give me the baby, I may as well carry him" (42). After issuing an invitation to the Wilsons for tea, the group assembles at the Bartons' home, where "Barton vibrated between the fire and the tea-table" while Mary assumed the task of preparing the eggs and the ham (53). All the while Mr. Wilson is trying "to quieten the other [baby] with bread soaked in milk." On another occasion Job Legh, the botanist, acts as "host and hostess too, for by a tacit agreement he . . . had assumed many of Margaret's little household duties" (197). The men in the novel combine traditionally male qualities of strength with traditionally female qualities of caring; conversely, Mary develops male traits of independence and toughness. The result is an enlargement of identity and an increase in sympathy, on both sides. For Gaskell, sympathy is the first step toward improving society, as sympathy enacts itself on both private and public levels.

Mary operates in both spheres, laboring within and outside the home. She believes and proves herself to be a capable, vital member of the family unit, one whose work is necessary to its functioning. Because she is known to be trustworthy, Mary is sent by her mother to ask Alice to join the company and to purchase food that will be served to the guests. After informing Alice of the occasion, "Mary ran off like a hare to fulfill what to a girl of thirteen, fond of power, was the more interesting part of her errand—the money-spending part. And well and ably did she perform her business" (52). As she prepares the food, Mary exhibits a "very comfortable portion of confidence in her own culinary powers" (53). After her mother's death, "All the money went through her hands, and the household arrangements were guided by her will and pleasure" (59). Taking a managerial role within the home serves as a training ground for Mary as she learns how to plan, execute, and perform business transactions. Scenes like these help Gaskell make her case for integrating women within the public sphere.

In addition to her instrumental role within the home, Mary performs labor outside it as well. In her account of Mary's search for a vocation, Gaskell is acknowledging the significance that work has in women's lives and insisting that they should make their own career decisions. John Barton recognizes the necessity of establishing Mary in an occupation: "Mary must do something" (61). Because of his distaste for factory work for women, Barton sees only two possibilities for Mary: going out to service and the dressmaking business, and "against the first of those, Mary set herself with all the force of her strong will" (61). Believing domestic servitude to be "a species of slavery," Barton is won over to his daughter's choice of occupation and endeavors to find a promising situation for her. His efforts, however, meet with no success, so the next day Mary takes charge of the situation, setting "out herself . . . and before night she had engaged herself as apprentice" (63). The conditions of her employment include the provision that she will work for two years without pay, and after this period of training, she is to receive a small quarterly salary.[15]

Yet despite the lack of economic benefits, Mary sees this plan as acceptable because it will allow her to maintain the independence to which she had become accustomed: "Mary was satisfied; and seeing this, her father was contented too" (63). The narrative shows Mary taking an active role in the process of securing an occupation for herself, realizing as she does that she can thereby have some control over the shape of her future.

Contrary to her contemporaries like Brontë and Eliot, who often present working girls as victimized, Gaskell wishes to show work's salutary and empowering effects. After a year passes, the narrator calls Mary a "blooming young work-girl," a description that suggests that Mary is thriving in her chosen work (65). Although she misses her mother, labor gives her the strength to assume an adult role; in fact, the narrator says, "She was far superior in sense and spirit to the mother she mourned" (64). Lansbury argues that Elizabeth Gaskell "saw a woman deriving strength and dignity from the ability to earn her own living."[16]

Through various characters in her novel, Gaskell addresses and dismisses the opposition, those who have serious reservations about women working. John Barton expresses the fear that work outside the home, especially factory work, can lead a young woman astray, reasoning that the ability to support herself might lead her to become vain and to overvalue finery, like his sister-in law Esther did. He also identifies as another potential hazard the freedom of movement that accompanies working.[17] Yet Gaskell does not share her character's fears. It is true that for a time Mary Barton accepts the attentions of Harry Carson, the factory owner's son, and entertains a vision of herself someday becoming a lady and "doing all the elegant nothings appertaining to ladyhood" (121). Yet her social ambitions are justified in part by her concern for her father's comfort; her rise in position would enable her to remove the cares that continually oppress him. Moreover, she does discover on her own the true state of her feelings—her preference for Jem Wilson—and acts accordingly, setting forth to Mr. Carson her decision to sever the association with him.[18] Wendy Craik comments on Mary's strength of character: "Far from helpless in her normal life, she has been a competent housekeeper, who has coped with sorrow, shortage of money, death, illness, overwork, sleepless nights, and her own personal dilemmas, all over a long period, during which she has also had to act independently without help or confidante."[19] Based on her own experience as a mother who watched a daughter, Meta, break off an engagement, Gaskell knows that a young woman could not be protected from the daily realities and dangers, from making her own mistakes, even by a parent. Gaskell makes clear her approval of female autonomy and self-reliance.

Gaskell juxtaposes her portrayal of Mary with her portrayal of the Carson sisters, daughters of the factory owner, in order to affirm the positive effects of labor. Mary's life of quiet purpose and usefulness contrasts sharply with the lives of the Carsons, who "like many similarly-situated young ladies, . . . did not exactly know what to do to while away the time until the tea-hour" (254). Gaskell criticizes a life of selfish leisure by presenting the Carsons as listless and sluggish. Having been at a dancing-party the night before, "One tried to read 'Emerson's Essays,' and fell asleep in the attempt; the other was turning over a parcel of new music, in order to select what she liked" (254-5). Sophy complains to her sister, "Oh, dear! how tired I am! . . . Are not you worn out, Helen?" To which Helen replies, "Yes; I am tired eough. One is good for nothing the day after a dance" (255). Their comfortable, easy lives are filled with dilettante pursuits that do not fit them for accomplishing anything.

As another case in point, their mother suffers the consequences of inactivity and serves as a prophetic example of what the future will likely hold for her daughters. Once a factory girl herself, Mrs. Carson was "as was usual with her . . . very poorly . . . indulging in the luxury of a head-ache. She was not well, certainly" (254). The narrator goes on to analyze the causes and possible cures for her condition:

> "Wind in the head," the servants called it. But it was but the natural consequence of the state of mental and bodily idleness in which she was placed. Without education enough to value the resources of wealth and leisure, she was so circumstanced as to command both. It would have done her more good than all the aether and sal-volatile she was daily in the habit of swallowing, if she might have taken the work of one of her own housemaids for a week; made beds, rubbed tables, shaken carpets, and gone out into the fresh morning air, without all the paraphernalia of shawl, cloak, boa, fur boots, bonnet, and veil, in which she was equipped before setting out for an "airing," in the closely shut-up carriage. (254)

Mrs. Carson has lived an idle life for so long that she is literally robbed of strength and purpose. These negative examples serve to heighten Mary's appeal to an audience that contained young working women who would identify with Mary as well as those who would identify more strongly with those of the managerial class, the Carsons.

Margaret Legh, Mary's friend, is another figure who demonstrates Gaskell's attitude toward women's work. Living with her grandfather, a skilled botanist, Margaret contributes to the family income by her spinning. Although she is gradually losing her vision, Margaret continues in her labor, even bringing sewing home to finish at night. Conscious of a responsibility to supplement the household funds, Margaret confides to Mary, "What I earn is a great help" (85).

However, sewing is not very rewarding to Margaret; it yields low pay, and, what is worse, her eyes suffer from the strain. Margaret is victimized by the financial necessity of performing hazardous work. The depiction of Margaret's labor is not only an attempt to stir the sympathy of Gaskell's middle-class audience, but also to emphasize the often heroic qualities of the working woman.

Nevertheless, Gaskell seems more interested in showing that women can find work enriching than in associating their work with their victimization. Aware that "some has one kind o' gifts, and some another," Margaret rightly recognizes that her gift is her voice, and she arranges to acquire some training with Jacob Butterworth, the singing weaver, who had been a "grand singer in his day" (181, 86). Margaret tells Mary about her efforts to develop her talent: "Well, I know'd him a bit, so I went to him, and said how I wished he'd teach me the right way o' singing; and he says I've a rare fine voice, and I go once a week, and take a lesson fra' him" (86). From a practical standpoint, Margaret's actions contain the promise of economic rewards: "He says I may gain ever so much money by singing" (86). When the opportunity presents itself, Margaret makes her musical debut, and "the managers said as how there never was a new singer so applauded" (136). Expressing her satisfaction about the situation, Margaret says proudly, "So I'm to sing again o' Thursday; and I got a sovereign last night, and am to have a half-a sovereign every night th' lecturer is at th' Mechanics'" (137). Music gives Margaret a sense of accomplishment and enhances her sense of identity. It also empowers her to assist Mary in her plan to save Jem Wilson from being charged with murder. Taking a sovereign from her savings, Margaret charges Mary: "You must take some of the mint I've got laid by in the old tea-pot" (320). Even after she loses a good deal of her sight, Margaret goes out alone about her business "as steadily as can be" (252). Her grandfather, at first afraid that she would be in danger, follows her and watches her make her way around the city; he soon becomes convinced that she knows how to take care of herself. Margaret effectively illustrates Gaskell's view that labor is empowering.

In spite of the independence and strong will she demonstrates in her actions, Margaret for the most part accepts the feminine ideal of passivity, advising her more impetuous friend, "You must just wait and be patient" when Mary regrets refusing Jem Wilson's offer of marriage (190). Mary is inclined to take action, saying, "Now I'd do anything" and asking "What can I do to bring him back to me? Should I write to him?" (189). Gaskell appears to prefer Mary's energy to Margaret's patience, giving Mary a central role in the plot while Margaret is confined to the periphery of the novel.

I have been arguing that Gaskell's central purpose in *Mary Barton* is to show how many of the problems surrounding work for women are inscribed in the life of a young working-class woman and to affirm the appropriateness of labor for women. The section of the novel that perhaps best illustrates Mary's competencies deals with the sequence of events leading up to Jem's trial. This section is given a significant amount of space in the novel, spanning several chapters. It is clear that Gaskell viewed these events as a crucial expression of Mary's identity, an identity that has been shaped by her participation in the workforce.

A kind of rescue sequence, often involving a trial, is a convention of the industrial novel. If we think back to what some of Gaskell's contemporaries do with these stock scenes, we will see just how different Gaskell's focus is. In *Sybil* Disraeli leads the plot to a moment when Sybil discovers that her father is about to be apprehended for his political activities; at this point she goes in search of her father, with every intention of warning him, but instead she arrives too late and collapses at a critical moment. This version of the scene turns on feminine weakness and ineptitude. Women cannot be accorded a place in public life, Disraeli suggests; they are too unreliable. George Eliot's treatment of a similar scene is a little closer to Gaskell's, but it too reveals serious reservations about women's participation in the public sphere. When Felix Holt is accused of leading a riot and charged with murder, Esther, aware that she has information that might help clear her lover, comes forward to present her evidence. Unlike Sybil, Esther is able to carry out her plan, but what Eliot stresses is the tremendous effort that it takes for Esther to speak. Despite the effort, Esther's words have relatively little effect on the turn of events; the words of men are necessary to acquit Felix Holt. These presentations of women's interventions imply that women are aliens in the public world of men; their attempts to join such a world are either harmful or merely ineffectual.

Gaskell comes to this scene with very different assumptions. Unlike her contemporaries, she makes a place for women in the public/political domain. Moreover, she inverts the power relations in the rescue sequence by placing Jem's life in Mary's capable hands. And she shows that women can be counted on. When Jem Wilson is held for murder, Mary's strength is put to its greatest test. Everything in her background—her early loss of a mother, her assumption of the role of breadwinner, and her support from loving neighbors—prepares her to take a crucial part in the vindication of her future husband. It is she who first devises a scheme to clear Jem: "He was with Will on Thursday night; walking a part of the way with him to Liverpool; now the thing is to lay hold on Will, and get him to prove this" (317). Her intention is met with doubt; even her friend Job Legh tells her not to "build too much on it" (317). Not to be deterred from her purpose, Mary responds, "Nothing you can say will daunt me, Job, so don't you go and try. You may help, but you cannot hinder me doing what I'm resolved on" (317).

Despite the negative reaction that she perceives from all those around her, Mary eventually proves herself to be correct in her assessment of Jem's innocence and shows herself capable of taking a leading role in his acquittal. The narrator says, "They respected her firmness of determination, and Job almost gave in to her belief, when he saw how steadfastly she was acting upon it" (317). The lawyer whom Job Legh enlists to defend Jem, a representation of patriarchy, is at first skeptical of Mary's powers to contribute to the case, believing that her "evidence would not be much either here or there" (322). Nevertheless, Mary persists in her plan, finally winning the admission from the previously dubious lawyer, "Ay, that's our only chance, I believe" and the confidence of Job Legh: "I must trust to her coming right. She's getten spirit and sense" (364, 368).

Mary's decision to help Jem requires from her quick judgment, physical stamina, and the courage to speak publicly. When Jem's mother is summoned to serve as a witness in the trial of her own son and faces the possibility of incriminating him, Mary takes the initiative of calling the doctor. After he examines her and expresses his opinion that a trip to Liverpool will not greatly harm her, Mary questions his diagnosis: "I did so hope you would say she was too ill to go" (331). The doctor is of an accommodating nature and agrees to take the opposite position: "It might certainly do her harm in her weak state" (332). Quick to seize the advantage, Mary continues, "And will you give me a certificate of her being unable to go, if the lawyer says we must have one?" (332). Thinking ahead and acting decisively, Mary demonstrates that she can carry out her purpose.

Mary's plan to rescue Jem also involves a difficult trip to Liverpool by railroad. The narrator makes it clear that such a form of travel carried with it a certain degree of inconvenience and turmoil: "Common as railroads are now in all places as a means of transit, and especially in Manchester, Mary had never been on one before; and she felt bewildered by the hurry, the noise of people, and bells, and horns" (343). Unaccompanied, Mary does not allow her uneasiness to hinder her from doing what she feels she must do. Despite her considerable "anxiety and fatigue, and several sleepless nights," Mary rouses herself once the train stops and asks a policeman for directions to the house where she believes Will Wilson to be staying (345). When she discovers that his ship has already sailed, she is dismayed, but she seizes on the small chance that his boat can be overtaken, asking the son of the landlady, "What must I do?" (349).

If the train were not bad enough, next Mary endures the experience of "rocking and tossing in a boat for the first time in her life, alone with two rough, hard-looking men" who agreed to try to catch up with the *John Cropper* (354). Without her temporary protector, the young boy who takes an interest in Mary's predicament, Mary withstands the gloomy, disheartening time in the boat, "sickening all the time with nervous fear" (356). At last the boat comes into sight, and "Mary stood up, steadying herself by the mast, and stretched out her arms, imploring the flying vessel to stay its course by that mute action" (357). Her gesture is seen, and although her throat was dry, and "all musical sound had gone out of her voice . . . in a loud harsh whisper she told the men her errand of life and death, and they hailed the ship" (358). All of her energy expended by the mental and physical strain of the day, Mary is befriended by the gruff old boatman, who takes her home to his wife and offers her shelter.

The day of the trial follows, when Mary, through sheer force of will, sheds all self-consciousness and speaks in Jem's behalf. The narrator's description of Mary initially focuses on her physical appearance, which reflects the emotional turmoil she is experiencing: "Many who were looking for mere flesh and blood beauty, mere colouring, were disappointed: for her face was deadly white, and almost set in its expression, while a mournful bewildered soul looked out of the depths of those soft, deep, grey eyes. But, others recognized a higher and stranger kind of beauty" (389).

The narrator comments that a bystander is haunted by her countenance, which reminds him of "some wild sad melody, heard in childhood; that . . . would perpetually recur with its mute imploring agony" (389). Up until this point, Mary is rendered in a conventional manner; as a young woman, her appearance is what is most significant about her, and she is inarticulate, unable to express herself.

Yet Gaskell does not allow Mary to be a slave to propriety and to conventional standards; she allows her to *speak*, thus resisting the role of passive observer of the events in her own life. Hilary Schor recognizes the political implications of this part of the novel: "the heroine's movement toward speech, her ability to 'own' her story, is as significant as her father's need to have his petition heard." [20] Realizing that she has a vital part to play in the proceedings, "suddenly she was roused, she knew not how or by what . . . . Her face flashed scarlet, and then paler than before. But in her dread of herself, . . . she exerted every power she had to keep in the full understanding of what was going on" (389).[21] Mary's plight is particularly difficult because she knows that her father, not Jem Wilson, is the real murderer and because she desires to protect her father as well as to see Jem cleared. Moreover, because her relationship with Harry Carson has a bearing on the case, providing a motive for the murder, Mary must endure the exposure of her private feelings before a crowd of witnesses. When the counsellor asks her which of the men she had preferred, Mary holds the power to proclaim the truth—a painful responsibility that she proves herself capable of.

> So, for an instant, a look of indignation contracted Mary's brow, as she steadily met the eyes of the impertinent counsellor. But, in that instant, she saw the hands removed of such intense love and woe,—such a deprecating dread of her answer; and suddenly her resolution was taken. The present was everything; the future, that vast shroud, it was maddening to think upon; but *now* she might own her fault, but *now* she might even own her love. Now, when the beloved stood thus, abhorred of men, there would be no feminine shame to stand between her and her avowal. (390)

Through her own strength, Mary imparts strength to Jem, who, after her testimony, "stood erect and firm, with self-respect in his attitude, and a look of determination on his face, which almost made it look noble" (392). When she is urged to leave the courtroom, she refuses to move and exclaims, "No! no! . . . . I must be here, I must watch that they don't hang him" (392). She manages to keep her composure until the arrival of Will, whose evidence will acquit Jem. This moment represents the culmination of Mary's labor on Jem's behalf. At this point, she collapses from the strain and is taken out of the court. While the prostration of the heroine from overwrought emotions is a stock scene in Victorian novels, it is important to note that Gaskell does not allow Mary to break down in a crisis. Having been thrust into situations that were foreign to her—on the train, on the water, in the court—she successfully performs her tasks and profoundly affects the outcome of events. Only after her part is done does she give in to the illness that had been coming on her throughout the trial. Later, when Jem resists going to his mother's because of his desire to stay with Mary, Job Legh admonishes him, "Never fear for Mary! She's young and will struggle through" (403).

After her exertions at the trial, Mary must take on another job: caring for and providing for her father in his final days. As she recovers her health, she gradually realizes that she must return to her home and confront her father. Disclosing her decision to Jem, she says, "Ah! but I must go home, Jem. I'll try and not fail now in what's right" (418). Moreover, she insists on going alone, even convincing Jem of her plan: "Then again he felt as if she were the best judge" (419). Once again in her old home, Mary is struck by her father's "abashed look, his smitten helplessness" (422). Taking the money that she had earned from her services as a witness, she "stole out to effect some purchases necessary for her father's comfort" (422). In essence, she becomes the parent, he the child, as she takes over all of the responsibilities for the household.[22]

The ending of the novel hints at new possibilities in a new environment. When Jem is thrown out of work, he asks Mary if she would be unhappy to leave Manchester and suggests Canada as the site of their future home. And even though Mary settles down into a domestic role as wife and mother, the foreign setting suggests freer, more flexible arrangements that allow for the development of Mary's talents. What emerges at the end is the picture of a marriage in which the husband acknowledges the intelligence and strength of his wife, qualities that assuredly grew out of her days as a young working girl who was largely left alone to take care of herself. Throughout the novel Gaskell draws attention to Mary's skill in dealing with crises, the inventiveness and fortitude that allow her to handle calamity with quiet competence. It is clear that Mary's experiences have fitted her for the complex trials of her life.

Mary Barton closes with a quiet family scene, in which letters from England are joyously received. They bring the news of the upcoming marriage of Margaret and Will and of the successful operation that restored Margaret's sight. The last image of the novel—a woman recovering her vision—is an interesting note to end on, for it is the image of a woman being empowered. Early in the novel, Margaret sings a moving song about the Oldham Weaver, and even Mary is amazed at the powerful performance of her friend.[23] Gaskell describes Mary's expression of wonder, her surprise that "the hidden power should not be perceived in the outward appearance" (74). In a way, this image is an apt one for the entire novel. Mary Barton, a seemingly simple factory girl, represents, despite her disarming looks, a powerful force, for she bears the ideological weight of her class, women who work and who become strong in their labor. In this novel, Mary is a persuasive argument for female vocation.

Notes

1. *Novels of the Eighteen Forties*, 202.

2. David observes that Gaskell was viewed by some "as a traitor to those people whom she hoped to enlighten" (*Fictions of Resolution in Three Victorian Novels*, 5).

3. Tillotson, in her important study, *Novels of the Eighteen Forties*, sees John Barton as the center of the novel and the character who provides unity in the work. Raymond Williams disagrees. See *Culture and Society, 1780-1950*.

4. Lansbury, *Elizabeth Gaskell: The Novel of Social Crisis*, 23.

5. Homans makes a convincing case for a new understanding of the inception of Gaskell's career when she argues that "the poem's vow never to forget the dead daughter continues to provide the impetus to write" and that "behind the myth of the writer as mother grieving over her son and directed by her husband's wisdom, who writes novels and publishes them immediately, lies hidden another writer who grieves alone over a daughter and writes a poem and a story she is reticent to publish" (*Bearing the Word: Language and Female Experience in Nineteenth Century Women's Writing*, 224). In *Elizabeth Gaskell*, Uglow gives a more detailed account of this sad event in Gaskell's life.

6. Martin recognizes Gaskell's interest in working women when she comments, "*Mary Barton* pleads for more than the working class. It asks for better opportunities for women" (*Petticoat Rebels*, 68).

7. Basch, *Relative Creatures: Victorian Women in Society and the Novel*, 180.

8. Williams, *Women in the English Novel, 1800-1900*, points out that nearly all the women in *Mary Barton* work outside of the home.

9. For some useful facts about the conditions faced by nineteenth century readers, I am indebted to Altick, *The English Common Reader: A Social History of the Mass Reading Public 1800-1900*, 87.

10. Tillotson, *Novels of the Eighteen Forties*, 23.

11. *Mary Barton*, 75; hereafter, page numbers are cited in parentheses in the text.

12. Beer correctly perceives that Gaskell always "presents energy attractively, even if it is overdone" (*Reader, I Married Him*, 168).

13. Beer observes that Mary is "almost an anticipation of the tomboy heroine of later Victorian fiction" (ibid., 165).

14. Stoneman has noted the positive characterization of nurturing men in Gaskell's novels: "What emerges from her work as a whole is that, at subsistence level, gender divisions are blurred: women exercise responsibility; men give basic nurturance" (*Elizabeth Gaskell*, 45).

15. Lansbury points out that in the popular mind dressmaking was a refined trade, while at the same time it was one of the poorest paid and most exploited (*Elizabeth Gaskell*, 57).

16. Lansbury, *Elizabeth Gaskell: The Novel of Social Crisis*, 31.

17. The novel does not bear out Gérin's claim that "repeatedly, in her writing [Gaskell] recurred to the theme of motherless girls . . . and ascribed all their misfortunes to this initial loss" (*Elizabeth Gaskell: A Biography*, 17).

18. Although Williams approves of Gaskell's treatment of the industrial suffering in *Mary Barton*, he denigrates the romance plot concerning Mary, Harry Carson, and Jem Wilson as "familiar and orthodox" and "of little lasting interest" (*Culture and Society*, 89). I would argue that these two modes are closely bound together. My understanding of the relationship of these seemingly separate plots is supported by Crosby, *The Ends of History*, who contends that women and their concerns have been perceived to be outside history because man "can know himself in history, find his origin there and project his end . . . only if there is something other than history." Crosby argues that women "are the unhistorical other of history" (1). According to Crosby, to imagine women as the "bearers of human affection" and "the medium of cultural transmission" is to exclude them from the historical realm (7).

19. Craik, *Elizabeth Gaskell and the English Provincial Novel*, 37.

20. See *Scheherezade in the Marketplace*. Uglow is aware that speech in *Mary Barton* involves struggle, observing that "the novel constantly returns to the difficulty of speaking." She points out that "again and again the characters fail to find the words they need" (*Elizabeth Gaskell*, 202).

21. Schor is insightful in finding a biographical parallel between Mary Barton's situation and her creator's: "Elizabeth Gaskell, the anonymous novelist who ducked under the breakfast table at the mere mention of *Mary Barton*, duplicates Mary's mixed humiliation and pride in her position at the center of the spectacle" (*Scheherezade in the Marketplace*, 41).

22. Schor suggests that Mary Barton "has moved beyond normal spheres of action for a woman in a novel: from private to public space, from silence to speech, from flirtation to love." She adds, "In a sense, she has won the battle over the novel that might have been called *John Barton*: it has become her story" (ibid., 38).

23. Spencer argues that the poetry of Ebenezer Elliott, the source of the mottos for four of Gaskell's chapters and the anonymous ballad "The Oldham Weaver," is included as a "means of letting working people's voices be heard" in the novel (*Elizabeth Gaskell*, 42).

Chapter 4

"It Needed to be a Woman,—So I Went": *North and South*

When she comes to *North and South* (1855), Gaskell turns her attention to a middle-class figure, one who would have been unfamiliar with the working-class life described in *Mary Barton*. Gaskell's intention in this second industrial novel is to examine labor problems from the other side, this time from the perspective of the managers and, more important, from the perspective of middle-class women. Hence she begins with a privileged young woman, whose life has sheltered her from the realities of earning a living. Initially an outsider, Margaret Hale moves in the course of the novel between the two classes, serving as an effective intermediary who promotes communication and understanding. Margaret comes to see herself as involved in the public sphere and abandons the position of observer for the position of participant. For Margaret, this means compromise and even pain, but at the same time an enlargement of identity. As she did in *Mary Barton*, Gaskell continues in *North and South* to collapse the distinction between the public and the private, revealing how they inevitably impinge on one another.

When pondering a title for the novel that eventually became *North and South*, Gaskell originally chose *Margaret Hale*, this time fully conscious from the start that her main interest lay in a female character.[1] (It was Dickens who suggested the title that finally stood, a version that clearly demonstrates his more abstract preoccupation with the conflict between the industrial and agrarian ways of life.) Again, as in *Mary Barton*, Gaskell allows her female protagonist to *act*; by *doing*, she defines herself and has an effect on the world around her.

The novel traces the maturation of Margaret Hale, whose comfortable life of privilege and freedom is replaced by the rigors of urban life in straitened circumstances. An overriding theme is Margaret's efforts to define her own work and to carry it out. While in *Mary Barton* Gaskell had explored the options available to a working-class woman, in *North and South* she confronts a more limited range of choices. The expectation of Victorian culture was that a middle-class woman had all of the work she would need within the context of her private familial roles.   In the process of discerning her proper work, Margaret rejects the notion that only domesticity is fitting to a lady and comes to understand that "she herself must one day answer for her own life and what she had done with it."[2]

Unlike Mary Barton, Margaret is given to reflection. Perhaps because of this quality, critics have responded favorably to her.[3] As she created the figure of Margaret, Gaskell was doubtless drawing on her own experiences as a young woman coming to industrial Manchester. Margaret's decisions about her life's work recall some of Gaskell's own and explain the strong sympathy that emanates from the novelist to the character.

From the outset, Gaskell is interested in representing her heroine as contrasting with conventional young women. The opening chapter, "Haste to the Wedding," contrasts Margaret and her cousin, Edith, establishing Margaret as deviating from Victorian norms of feminine behavior in several important ways. The first scene is highly suggestive, beginning with Margaret's discovery that Edith is fast asleep on the sofa: Margaret's immediate reaction is to awaken her. Lying "curled up" in the drawing-room, "looking very lovely in her white muslin and blue ribbons," Edith is remarkable only for her decorative value. In her somnolence, Edith resembles the Carson sisters, whose days are largely spent dressing for, going to, and recovering from balls. Gaskell often links daytime drowsiness in her women characters with an indolent, luxurious existence. Likewise, an inability to sleep at night suggests a lack of activity. Later in the novel, when Margaret is asked by her mother if she finds the beds comfortable, Margaret answers, "I've never thought about my bed at all . . . . I'm so sleepy at night, that if I only lie down anywhere, I nap off directly" (261). In confirmation of the impression Edith immediately invites, the narrator mentions her objection to some arrangement regarding her wedding, but goes on to say that "although she was a spoiled child she was too careless and idle to have a strong will of her own, and gave way" (36). Edith appears infantile, taking a nap in midday, like a child, and leaving the planning of her own wedding to her mother. Throughout the novel, Margaret is played off against Edith, who embodies the Victorian norm for femininity. In contrast, Margaret seeks a realm of action that will challenge her and make use of her talents. When she hears her aunt calling for Edith, Margaret explains that her cousin is asleep and asks, "Is it anything I can do?" (38). Victorian society does not offer her many opportunities for fulfilling labor; throughout the novel she must search for and claim her own work.

Gaskell makes it clear that Margaret is not content with the prospect of marriage as the primary end of her existence.[4] The first thing we see her do is stand in for Edith, modeling the regal shawls that "would have half-smothered Edith" (39).[5] Smiling when she sees herself in such splendor, Margaret views the finery merely as a costume, not as a true expression of her selfhood.

"Trying on" Edith's identity, she rejects her cousin's set of values, complaining to Henry Lennox about the complexities of wedding preparations, "the never-ending commotion about trifles that had been going on for more than a month past" (41). When Lennox laughs, dismissing her point, Margaret persists; "a sense of indescribable weariness of all the arrangements for a pretty effect . . . oppressed her just now" (41). Margaret defines herself against the Victorian standard that would require women to be continuously on display as candidates in the marriage market and conceives of new possibilities for herself and other women.[6]

Margaret's dissatisfaction grows out of a stifling environment that fails to summon her to action or use. Although Margaret displays more depth of character and intellect than her cousin, she lives a similarly privileged life in a country parsonage, taking her holidays at her Aunt Shaw's house. At the same time, she is reluctant to break out of what she already knows. In response to a question by Henry Lennox about the likelihood of her gardening at Helstone, Margaret replies, "I am afraid I shan't like such hard work" (43). At Helstone her days are filled with visits to the rural folk—taking them food, reading to them, nursing their children—and frequent long walks in appreciation of the natural world. In her visits Margaret does perform useful social work, but her position in relation to her neighbors is that of gracious patroness. She plays the part of a Lady Bountiful, conferring her benevolence on her father's parishioners. As such, she is merely filling a role that falls to her by virtue of being the daughter of a minister.[7]

It takes several crises to extricate Margaret from this narrow field of action in a static environment and to transfer her into a setting where she can find her own work. The first is her father's announcement that he can no longer be a minister in the Church of England and the consequent necessity of leaving Helstone. Her father's decision to confide in Margaret about his intentions throws more adult responsibility on her; moreover, he even confers the task of enlightening Mrs. Hale on his daughter. A process of individuation and distancing begins when Margaret is forced to evaluate her father's actions and sees weakness in his failure to tell his own wife about his spiritual crisis. After breaking the news to her mother, Margaret takes a leading role in the planning involved in the move to Milton. Reflecting on her former life, she realizes the irreversible change that has occurred: "She felt that it was a great weight suddenly thrown upon her shoulders. Four months ago, all the decisions she needed to make were what dress she would wear for dinner, and to help Edith to draw out the lists of who should take down whom in the dinner parties at home. Nor was the household in which she lived one that called for much decision" (85). Within the patriarchal family, Margaret has been sheltered and protected from difficult decisions; the rearrangement of the family power structure is necessary before Margaret can begin to see her vocation in life.

In the absence of strong parental models, Margaret assumes the task of making decisions, as well as carrying them out. It becomes Margaret's responsibility to arrange the transition to Milton in such a way as to cause the least inconvenience to her mother; in an effort to spare her fatigue, Margaret suggests leaving her mother and Dixon, her maid, at Heston, a quiet bathing place, while she and her father go to look at houses. Her father agrees to her plan, allowing Margaret to decide that Dixon would remain in the household. This step taken, "now Margaret could work, and act, and plan in good earnest" (86). When the day of the move arrives, it is Margaret, "calm and collected," with "her large grave eyes observing everything," who supervises the men who had come to help (89). She reasons to herself: "If she gave way, who was to act?" (89). When decisions had to be made concerning lodgings, it is again Margaret who makes them, telling her father, "I have planned it all" and exclaiming, "I am overpowered by the discovery of my own genius for management" (97, 98). Not only does she select the house, but she also determines how each room will be occupied, taking into account individual needs and preferences. For the first time in her life, Margaret takes a leading role in directing the shape of events as they relate to her family.

Margaret's newfound authority begins to extend outward, as she interacts with those outside her family.[8] When the family servant takes too much freedom, criticizing Mr. Hale and trying to keep Mrs. Hale's medical condition a secret, Margaret uses her authoritative demeanor to secure her own position as daughter of the house. Responding to a negative remark about her father, Margaret says firmly, "Dixon! you forget to whom you are speaking," thereby gaining respect from Dixon, who "would have resented such words from anyone less haughty and determined in manner" (83). Margaret's "straight, fearless, dignified presence" helps her command respect and wield authority, even over men (99).[9] Upon arriving at the hotel where the Hales are staying temporarily, John Thornton, the wealthy manufacturer, is rather taken aback when he meets Margaret for the first time: "Mr. Thornton was in habits of authority himself, but she seemed to assume some kind of rule over him at once" (99). Thornton immediately realizes that Margaret is no ordinary woman and responds to her powerful presence. Similarly, when the doctor comes to see her mother, Margaret quickly takes over, ushering him in "with an air of command" and extracting from him the truth about her mother's illness (173). Understanding that Margaret needs to know the facts and that she is capable of handling them, the doctor is honest with her and even expresses admiration for the young woman: "That's what I call a fine girl! thought Dr. Donaldson . . . . Who would have thought that little hand could have given such a squeeze? . . . Another, who had gone that deadly colour, could never have come round without either fainting or hysterics. But she wouldn't do either—not she!" (174-5). Margaret's successful management of the workload that falls to her contributes to her aura of competence, an aura that other people acknowledge.

Her mother's terminal illness is another major crisis that requires Margaret's energies and shows her what she is capable of. After revealing to her mother that she knows about Mrs. Hale's condition, Margaret requests permission to act as nurse. At first meeting resistance, she finally convinces her mother of her competence, scoffing at Dixon's inaccurate image of her young mistress: "She thought, I suppose, that I was one of those poor sickly women who like to lie on rose leaves, and be fanned all day" (176). Caring for her mother requires of Margaret physical as well as emotional stamina, particularly as she cannot share the trial with her father. Margaret tells Dixon, "He could not bear it as I can" (177). In spite of her sorrow, as she steps out for a walk, hoping to collect herself for what lies ahead, Margaret feels her powers surging forth: "Her step grew lighter; her lip redder" (180). As she relates these scenes in which Margaret tends her ailing mother, Gaskell is responding to her culture's association of true womanliness with the sick chamber. However, in contrast to Sarah Ellis, who believes that nursing is the sphere within which true womanliness develops, Gaskell does not glorify the self-abnegation that is a requirement of tending the sick. Nor does she sentimentalize it as anything less than arduous, draining labor.[10] Margaret needs strength to be an effective nurse, and she develops into an even stronger woman as a result of the experience. Instead of presenting her character as enervated by the demands of the work, Gaskell presents Margaret as energized.

Faced with the necessity of performing physical work, Margaret comes to believe that labor is not incompatible with being a lady. She is even capable of joking about the social definitions, commenting when she sits down after a long day that she is "no longer Peggy the laundry-maid, but Margaret Hale the lady" (115). When her mother takes her remark as an expression of discontent, she insists, "I don't mind ironing, or any kind of work, for you and papa. I am myself a born lady through it all, even though it comes to scouring a floor, or washing dishes" (116). Margaret even begins to be ashamed of the image of herself as idle lady that she presents to society. After a dinner at the Thorntons, she tells her father that she "felt like a great hypocrite to-night, sitting there in my white silk gown, with my idle hands before me, when I remembered all the good, thorough, house-work they had done to-day. They took me for a fine lady, I'm sure" (221-2). Living in Milton gradually leads Margaret to view herself as a woman who works.

Moreover, her friendship with a working-class woman, Bessy Higgins, supports Margaret as she gradually moves toward her chosen work.[11] With her rural background, Margaret is at first somewhat shocked at the manners of the urban working class. As she goes out on the streets of Milton on her errands, she repeatedly falls in with the factory workers, who "came rushing along, with bold, fearless faces, and loud laughs and jests" (110). In fact, the narrator says, "the tones of their unrestrained voices, and their carelessness of all common rules of street politeness, frightened Margaret a little at first" (110). For the first time, Margaret is exposed to casual comments about her appearance, and her first response is indignation. Yet her friendship with one workman, Nicholas Higgins, and his daughter Bessy helps her shed her prim aloofness and strengthens her as she faces difficulties.[12] In order for Margaret to be effective in her new environment, she must learn to accommodate herself to the working-class mores, which are new to her. The first step in this process is to form a close bond with an individual working-class family.

Margaret initially assumes that the kind of patronage she conferred on her neighbors at Helstone will characterize her relations at Milton. Yet her first attempt to establish herself as patroness is received with suspicion, not gratitude. When Margaret asks the Higginses their names and address, she meets with the response, "Whatten yo' asking for?" (112). At this point she is forced to explain her motives, and she does so hesitatingly: "I thought—I meant to come and see you" (113). From this incident Margaret begins to realize that she must learn a new set of social relationships.

Through Bessy Higgins, Margaret discovers the value of female friendship based on shared experience, which involves for both women sacrifice and work. As Bessy shares the details of her grueling life with her new friend, Margaret recalls with some shame those former days when "other people were hard at work in some distant place, while [she] just sat on the heather and did nothing" (145). Bessy's work in the mill has resulted in her ill health, as the fluff from the cotton gradually filled her lungs. From Bessy's point of view, the situation was inevitable:

> But our factory was a good one on the whole; and a steady likely set o' people; and father was afeard of letting me go to a strange place, for though yo' would na think it now, many a one then used to call me a gradely lass enough. And I did na like to be reckoned nesh and soft, and Mary's schooling were to be kept up, mother said, and father he were always liking to buy books, and go to lectures o' one kind or another—all which took money—so I just worked on till I shall ne'er get the whirr out o' my ears, or the fluff out o' my throat i' this world. (146-7)

After asking Bessy her age and discovering that they are both nineteen, Margaret reflects on the contrast between them. Yet Margaret is able to empathize with Bessy's pain, for she has her own sorrows, and it is the obligation to work for their families that forms the basis of their friendship.

This friendship with a working-class woman teaches Margaret that "God has made us so that we must be mutually dependent" (169). Margaret's recognition that there are commonalities that bind her and Bessy leads her to an understanding of the benefits she receives from her less fortunate friend. On a visit to the Higginses, Bessy describes what a strike will mean for her family, and in the process Margaret gets perspective on her own difficulties. As she is leaving, Margaret says, "You have done me good, Bessy" (187). When Bessy expresses surprise at the comment, Margaret explains, "Yes. I came here very sad, and rather too apt to think my own cause for grief was the only one in the world. And now I hear how you have had to bear for years, and that makes me stronger" (187). Bessy becomes aware of her contribution as well, for she exclaims, "Bless yo'! I thought a' the good-doing was on the side of gentlefolk" (187).

On another occasion, Bessy advises Margaret before she attends a dinner given by the Thorntons at Marlborough Mills, preparing her for the kind of society that she is likely to be thrown into there. Aware—as Margaret is not—that the Thorntons "visit wi' a' th' first folk in Milton," Bessy is amazed when Margaret tells her that she has been invited to dine (199). "With an anxious look at Margaret's print gown," Bessy informs her friend, "Them ladies dress so grand!" (200). As a result of Bessy's counsel, Margaret decides to wear her white silk, a choice that Bessy approves: "That'll do!" (200). Gaskell describes in positive terms this friendship to which both persons contribute; female solidarity—across and within classes—is a theme that recurs in her fiction. Such solidarity is often crucial as it empowers each character to do her own particular work.

The longer Margaret lives in Milton, the more she adapts to the industrial setting; her attitudes and her behavior change as she earns a right to speak for the workers. Evidence of such a shift involves her use of language.[13] In a conversation with her mother, Margaret suggests asking Mary Higgins to help when her brother Frederick comes to visit. Arguing that "she is very slack of work, and is a good girl, and would take pains to do her best," Margaret is reprimanded by her mother for using "horrid Milton words" such as the expression "slack of work" (301). Margaret defends herself by saying, "if I live in a factory town, I must speak factory language when I want it," and by pointing out that local words are extremely expressive and efficient (302). As an example she cites the term "knobstick," which would require an entire explanatory sentence. Margaret's appreciation—and appropriation—of the language of the working class demonstrates her willingness to assume their point of view.

Along with the speech of the workers, Margaret comes to accept their customs. When she learns that her friend Bessy has died, Margaret is asked if she would like to see the body. Her first reaction is "But she's dead! . . . I never saw a dead person. No! I would rather not" (278). However, after she learns that Bessy had requested to be buried in something of hers and that Bessy would have "thought it a great compliment" for her to come and see her in death, Margaret relents: "Yes, perhaps I may. Yes, I will. I'll come before tea" (278). When a new situation arises, Margaret questions her own middle-class notions about appropriateness and demonstrates a willingness to adopt the values of her friends.

At the same time, she does not accept their actions unquestioningly, but reserves the right to make judgments for herself. In a conversation about the strike, Margaret asks probing questions about the Union. Nicholas Higgins reluctantly discloses the methods used to pressure workers into joining the organization:

> Well! If a man doesn't belong to th' Union, them as works next looms has orders not to speak to him—if he's sorry or ill it's a' the same; he's out o' bounds; he's none o' us. I' some places them's fined who speaks to him. Yo' try that, miss; try living a year or two among them as looks away if yo' look at 'em; try working within two yards o' crowds o' men, who, yo' know, have a grinding grudge at yo' in their hearts—to whom if yo' say yo're glad, not an eye brightens, nor a lip moves,—to whom if your heart's heavy, yo' can never say nought, because they'll ne'er take notice on your sighs or sad looks . . . —just yo' try that, miss—ten hours for three hundred days, and yo'll know a bit what th' Union is. (295-6)

In reaction to Higgins' description, Margaret exclaims, "Why! . . . what tyranny this is . . . . And you belong to the Union! And you talk of the tyranny of the masters!" (296). A little later, when Margaret acts as a mediator between the masters and the workers, her effectiveness stems in part from this readiness to articulate the flaws in the reasoning of both sides.

Margaret's confrontation with injustice on behalf of her brother likewise propels her into the public sphere as she works to vindicate him. On board the *Russell*, Frederick had tolerated the tyranny of the commanding officer, Captain Reid, until his "imperiousness in trifles" led to the senseless death of a sailor (152). At that point, a mutiny broke out, and, as a result, Frederick was branded a traitor. Margaret mentions the possibility of clearing Frederick, asking, "If he came and stood his trial, what would be the punishment? Surely, he might bring evidence of his great provocation" (154). When Frederick comes home to be with his dying mother, it is Margaret who initiates a plan to acquit her brother. Arguing that he might "show how [his] disobedience to authority was because that authority was unworthily exercised," Margaret rouses Frederick to action (325). At first dubious of his chances, he asks how his witnesses might be summoned as they are all sailors, scattered over the seas. In the face of obstacles, Margaret suggests proceeding, asking her brother if it is not possible that witnesses who could speak for him might be assembled. She finally suggests that he consult a lawyer concerning his chances of exculpation and names Henry Lennox. "[W]arming up into her plan," Margaret proposes that Frederick go to London the next evening by a night-train and sits down to compose a note to Henry Lennox explaining the situation. Indeed Margaret guides the entire family discussion regarding Frederick's welfare. Margaret's assessment of Frederick's chances proves to be correct, for Lennox agrees that acquittal is possible with credible witnesses. And when it becomes too dangerous for Frederick to stay any longer in England, Margaret, at considerable risk, accompanies him to the station.

In these scenes Gaskell is careful not to present Margaret as immune to the complexities and dangers of operating in the public sphere. Nor does she create an easy solution to Frederick's problem. As she keeps her brother company on his way to the train, a drunken man accosts Margaret, pushing her roughly, and seizes her brother by the collar. Frederick manages to trip the assailant and jump on the train, but Margaret is left to handle the long-reaching consequences of the encounter. When a policeman shows up at her door and informs her that the man has died and that an inquest will be held, Margaret is put in the awkward position of either having to admit her presence on the train, thereby implicating her brother, or to tell a lie, thereby compromising her ethics. In an effort to protect Frederick, Margaret lies, and this lie follows her, for a while damaging her relationship with John Thornton. Moreover, the witnesses who are needed to acquit her brother are never found, and he is forced to be a permanent exile. By emphasizing the painful choices and misunderstandings that are concomitant with acting in the public domain, Gaskell departs from domestic ideology, which holds that women can magically purify and feminize the public sphere.

In this part of the novel, Margaret's private relationship with her brother has public consequences: Margaret lies to a police officer, a representative of the state, thereby alienating her admirer, John Thornton, who sees her behavior as confirming some kind of illicit relationship. Feeling degraded by her capitulation to falsehood, Margaret torments herself for having lacked the courage to tell the truth. Yet Gaskell clearly intends for the reader to sympathize with Margaret; after all, she does lie to protect a family member, not to protect herself. Moreover, Margaret is not forced into a repetition of the lie; John Thornton intervenes with the coroner and forestalls any further inquiry. One implication here is that women cannot remain isolated in the privatized space of domesticity, and that acting in the public realm will inevitably require ethical compromises. This experience with Frederick is Margaret's initiation into public life; given the Victorian expectations for women, shame and self-reproach are plausible responses on her part. Despite her sense of mortification, Margaret does not retreat from participation in the world of men.

Margaret's most important work in the novel involves her efforts to settle a standoff between the owner of the mill and its hands. It is because of her new friendship with a working-class family that Margaret develops an interest in labor relations and attempts to understand the positions represented by both sides when a dispute breaks out. Realizing that she has a part to play in this situation, she takes up the issue with John Thornton, forcing him to examine and justify his own actions.[14] In a discussion over an impending strike, she inquires why he does not inform his workers about the reasons for current trade problems. He, on the other hand, defends his right to withhold explanations from his employees, asking Margaret, "Do you give your servants reasons for your expenditure, or your economy in the use of your own money?" (164). In this interchange—and others that follow—Margaret views the workers as adults to be treated fairly and respectfully. When the strike breaks out, Margaret urges

Thornton to face them "like a man" and encourages him to "speak to [his] workmen as if they were human beings" (232). Thornton's very terminology for his workers, whom he calls "hands," suggests separation and compartmentalization. Instead of seeing them in their full humanity, Thornton thinks only of their working parts, their hands, which can produce marketable goods. John Thornton's tendency to view the issue from a business point of view—regarding the workforce as a purely economic unit—is corrected by Margaret, who brings the values of private life into the discussion.

Yet realizing that the private sphere cannot remain inviolate from the conflicts in the public sphere, Margaret undertakes the task of representing the interests of the workers, using her influence with Thornton to try to improve their working conditions. As she argues with Thornton, she expresses her disapproval of the masters' desire that their hands "be merely tall, large children—living in the present moment—with a blind unreasoning kind of obedience" (166). Making a case for the necessity of recognizing the workers as adult equals, Margaret tells the story of a rich man in Nuremberg who attempted to shield his only son from evil but who "had made the blunder of bringing him up in ignorance and taking it for innocence" (168). She employs this analogy to point out the consequences of keeping the workers ignorant of decisions made by management.[15] Supporting more equal relations between workers and employers, Margaret sympathizes with the plight of the workers, who are powerless to negotiate with management. Believing that "loyalty and obedience to wisdom and justice are fine; but it is still finer to defy arbitrary power, unjustly and cruelly used," Margaret nevertheless views the strike as defeating the purposes of the oppressed (154). Instead, she proposes communication between both sides as the more promising solution to their problems.

As Margaret labors on behalf of her brother and on behalf of the workers, she enters territory considered by Victorian society to be off limits to women.[16] Margaret finds the areas that are socially defined as appropriate to women both trivial and confining. After the dinner party given by the Thorntons, Margaret tells her father her impressions of the evening:

> I was very much interested by what the gentlemen were talking about, although I did not understand half of it. I was quite sorry when Miss Thornton came to take me to the other end of the room, saying she was sure I was uncomfortable at being the only lady among so many gentlemen. I had never thought about it, I was so busy listening; and the ladies were so dull, papa—oh, so dull! Yet I think it was clever too. It reminded me of our old game of having each so many nouns to introduce into a sentence . . . . Why, they took nouns that were signs of things which gave evidence of wealth,—housekeepers, under-gardeners, extent of glass, valuable lace, diamonds, and all such things; and each one formed her speech so as to bring them all in, in the prettiest accidental manner possible. (221)

Margaret's words echo her author's, who said in a letter that she found men to be very interesting and who once called women who did not take advantage of the space made available for them at a public lecture "stupid creatures" (Letters 633, 279). Like Gaskell, Margaret finds the company of men congenial and stimulating, and, like Gaskell, she gets impatient at the ladies for their lack of interest in topics that engage her. Through Margaret, Gaskell makes a case for the right of women to participate in discussions on topics thought to be "masculine," suggesting that women can make important contributions to such debates.[17]

Conversely, Gaskell supports the movement of men into the woman's arena, the work of the home. When Frederick comes home, Margaret discovers that shared work can create a profound bond between the sexes. Their mother asleep, Margaret prepares to offer refreshments to her brother. His response to her shows her the value of male partnership: "When all was ready, Margaret opened the study door, and went in like a serving-maiden, with a heavy tray held in her extended arms. She was proud of serving Frederick. But he, when he saw her, sprang up in a minute, and relieved her of her burden. It was a type, a sign, of all the coming relief which his presence would bring. The brother and sister arranged the table together, saying little, but their hands touching, and their eyes speaking" (311). Later in the evening, Frederick ministers to his parents, delicately using his conversational powers to cheer his father and to relieve his mother's pain. "His patient devotion and watchfulness came into play, and made him an admirable nurse" (313). The traditionally female roles of servant and nurse are assumed competently by Frederick, whose philosophy is "Do something, my sister, do good if you can; but, at any rate, do something" (315). The relationship between brother and sister involves a kind of alternation of support; after their mother dies, Frederick breaks down, and it is again Margaret who must hold the family together. As Coral Lansbury notes, "Elizabeth Gaskell was aware that women, like men, shared common human responsibilities."[18]

It is up to Margaret to persuade John Thornton to accept help from herself, a woman; in so doing, Margaret teaches him about new social possibilities.[19] Again, Gaskell is inverting conventional notions of gender by showing a woman instructing a man.[20] Regarded among his fellows as a "man of great force of character; of power in many ways," Thornton at first resists Margaret's attempts to involve herself in the struggle between workers and employers (216). Yet another woman—Thornton's own mother—precedes Margaret in the demonstration of women's abilities. A stern, tough-minded woman, Mrs. Thornton informs Margaret of the possibility of a strike, without minimizing the dangers of such an occurrence: "Milton is not the place for cowards. I have known the time when I have had to thread my way through a crowd of white, angry men, all swearing they would have Makinson's blood as soon as he ventured to show his nose out of his factory; and he, knowing nothing of it, some one had to go and tell him, or he was a dead man; and it needed to be a woman,—so I went" (162). When an ominous crowd gathers outside the Thorntons' house, threatening the lives of the wealthy family inside, Mrs. Thornton refuses her son's suggestion to go into the back rooms, insisting "where you are, there I stay" (230). Her steadiness and resolution in the face of personal danger attest to the fitness of women to perform in a crisis.

Following the maternal example, Margaret chooses to make a public appearance before the mob. When Margaret senses that "in an instant, all would be uproar," she lifts the iron bar of the door and throws the door open wide, making herself perfectly visible to the mob. Relying on a woman's presumed inviolability to shield Thornton, she steps between him and his enemies. When the men are on the brink of violence, she takes a final, desperate action: she throws her arms around Thornton to shelter him.[21] When he tells her, "Go away . . . . This is no place for you," she counters, "It is. You did not see what I saw" (234). A pebble grazes Margaret's head, knocking her down, and she suffers the humiliation of being misunderstood for her effort to defend Thornton, but, in retrospect, she expresses scorn for conventional standards for femininity: "I would do it again, let who will say what they like of me. If I saved one blow, one cruel, angry action that might otherwise have been committed, I did a woman's work" (247).

When Margaret takes the powerful position of public mediator, she relinquishes her immunity from the scrutiny of many eyes and makes herself the subject of all kinds of disturbing speculations. Gaskell is explicit on this point: "If she thought her sex would be a protection,—if, with shrinking eyes she had turned away from the terrible anger of these men, in any hope that ere she looked again they would have paused and reflected, and slunk away, and vanished,—she was wrong" (234). Margaret is stared at, physically wounded, and finally proposed to—all as a consequence of her presence on a public stage. In her treatment of John Thornton's response to Margaret's act, Gaskell indicates the interpenetration of the public and private. Interestingly, Margaret asserts the public nature of her behavior while Thornton wishes to see her behavior as only an expression of private feeling. When he declares his love to her, she immediately resists, denying that her conduct "was a personal act" and insisting that "any woman, worthy of the name of woman, would come forward to shield . . . a man in danger" (253). He, on the other hand, claims the "right of expressing [his] feelings" (253). In this scene gender distinctions get turned completely upside down as the woman takes a public stand on behalf of a man, and a man speaks for romance, the center of the private world. What is even more interesting is that Gaskell validates both perspectives; Margaret's act is definitely political, but it is, at least on a subconscious level, personal as well. As a result of Thornton's declaration, Margaret is forced to confront her unacknowledged feelings about him. The memory of Margaret's action makes her even more desirable to him, and her preoccupation with his reaction to her leads her to self-understanding. One implication here seems to be that the benefits of acting in the public sphere will ultimately outweigh the costs.

Although Thornton resists the idea that women have a public function, he is more willing to make an exception for an exceptional woman like Margaret, who comes to see herself as an agent of reconciliation and change. Recognizing that if they met face to face, the men would respect each other and be able to work out their differences, Margaret suggests that Nicholas Higgins go to John Thornton to seek work at his factory. Because Higgins has been a leader in the Union, Thornton at first sends Higgins away, instructing him to tell the woman who sent him to "mind [her] own business" and declaring that "women are at the bottom of every plague in this world" (403, 398). Dismayed to learn that Margaret was the woman who sent him and that his words had been repeated to her, Thornton changes his mind, and actually follows Higgins to his own home, asking, "Will you take work with me?" (405). The encounter ends with Higgins offering a thank you, an act that he says is "a deal fro' me," and Thornton extending his hand, likewise saying "this is a deal from me" (405). Thornton accepts Margaret's assessment of the public situation and moves toward a possible solution by offering work to Higgins, thereby initiating a system in which managers and workers will form personal relationships.

Gaskell sets in motion a series of events that invert conventional expectations involving both gender and class: first, she represents a woman—rather than a man—initiating a change in the way public affairs are conducted; then she represents a manager seeking to placate a worker—rather than the other way around. Here Gaskell is showing how change breeds more change and how a shift in the power structure can lead to more equitable social arrangements. As a result of Margaret's intervention, a personal truce between two former antagonists leads to change: after a later visit to Higgins, Thornton is made aware of the lack of food and schooling that is common among his workers and decides to educate some children in whom Higgins takes an interest and to create a system in his factory whereby the men are fed adequately and cheaply. In both these acts, Margaret's influence is present, for they are both caring, nurturing gestures toward meeting the needs of workers. The workers respond in turn by inviting Thornton to share a meal with them, and the formerly aloof master says, "I am getting really to know some of them now, and they talk pretty freely before me" (446). When a period of bad trade leads to significant losses for Thornton, the workers rally to his support, staying overtime, unknown to anyone, to get the work done. Thornton recognizes the value of this new set of relations with his workers, telling a member of Parliament, "My only wish is to have the opportunity of cultivating some intercourse with the hands beyond the mere 'cash nexus' . . . . I have arrived at the conviction that no mere institution, however wise, . . . can attach class to class as they should be attached, unless the working out of such institutions bring the individuals of the different classes into actual personal contact" (525).

The resolution of the novel continues the pattern of inversion and points to the inextricable union of the public and the private through the marriage of the central characters. In the final chapters Margaret finds herself with that windfall so common to Victorian heroines: a legacy. This sudden possession of ample funds of money puts her to a moral test: will she relinquish a life committed to serious purpose for a life of pleasant ease? Hours by the seaside give Margaret a chance to examine her life and to make some decisions about the shape of her future.

> When they returned to town, Margaret fulfilled one of her seaside resolves, and took her life into her own hands. Before they went to Cromer, she had been as docile to her aunt's laws as if she were still the scared little stranger who cried herself to sleep that first night in the Harley street nursery. But she had learnt, in those solemn hours of thought, that she herself must one day answer for her own life, and what she had done with it; and she tried to settle that most difficult problem for women, how much was to be utterly merged in obedience to authority, and how much might be set apart for freedom in working. (508)

At this point, Margaret occupies a position of power: she has money just when it is needed by Thornton. As a result of the strike and his subsequent engagement of Irish workers, he is unable to complete some of the large orders that would have helped him turn a profit. In addition, a period of bad trade causes the value of stocks to fall and Thornton's assets to be cut in half. When Thornton is forced to prepare himself for the wreck of his fortunes and the loss of his factory, Margaret steps in, at the risk of rejection, and offers to make her money available to Thornton so that he can continue to run Marlborough Mills and, more important, continue in the work toward reform she instigated.

Margaret's gesture is not impulsive or spontaneous. Nor is it motivated by a desire to play benefactress or to make a grand dramatic scene. Having been estranged from Thornton for over a year, Margaret has no reason to believe that there is any hope of a relationship between them, as she thinks that she has forever lost his respect. Because she wishes to support the changes he has instigated in his business practices, she consults a lawyer about a plan to lend him the amount of money he needs to continue running Marlborough Mills. Margaret does not even intend to be present when the plan is explained to Thornton, but when Henry Lennox does not keep his appointment and John Thornton has been kept waiting for nearly an hour, she has no choice but to explain the legal proceedings that she has set in motion. Aware that Thornton might resist her assistance, Margaret is careful to present her offer as "a mere business arrangement, in which the principal advantage would be on her side" (529).

Gaskell skillfully negotiates the interplay between private motives and public actions in this concluding scene. The reader is certain that Margaret's gesture is a sincere effort to continue the public work that she has been involved with in Milton; nevertheless the reader is also aware that Margaret harbors deep feelings for John Thornton. Within this context, Margaret takes an action that may be understood as simultaneously political and personal, making an offer that Thornton must read correctly in its fullness if he is to receive all of its benefits. Gaskell puts the future for the couple in Margaret's hands; it is she who enables Thornton to make a declaration. Having been instructed by Margaret, Thornton is quick to perceive the personal motive and responds in kind, simply calling her name. The interesting part of the interchange has to do with Gaskell's repeated references to silence throughout the scene. After Thornton says "Margaret" once, there is a pause; after the second time, another. Finally, he warns her, "If you do not speak—I shall claim you as my own in some strange presumptuous way.—Send me away at once, if I must go" (529). Again, "they both kept silence" (529). When the once-arrogant Margaret murmurs, "Oh, Mr. Thornton, I am not good enough," Thornton echoes her sentiment, imploring her, "Don't mock my own deep feeling of unworthiness," and again they sit in silence. These silences suggest that Margaret and Thornton have learned to understand each other, and that this understanding at times transcends language.

What follows is a silent replay of an earlier scene between them: Thornton removes her hands from her face and places her arms "as they had once before been placed to protect him from the rioters" (530). This tableau reenacts the public scene, but this time on a personal basis. Moments of silence are punctuated by language that hints of private significations. Thornton presents some dead roses that he has been carrying in his pockets and asks Margaret if she recognizes them. When she identifies them as from her former home, Helstone, Thornton explains that he made a trip there, when he saw no prospect of ever winning Margaret, just to see "the place where Margaret grew to what she is" (530). This reference to a search for clues into Margaret's identity is promising, for it suggests Thornton's acknowledgment of her complexity and his attentiveness to her. In this novel, Gaskell implies that the marriage between Margaret and John Thornton will be a partnership in which both will work together, in the private and the public spheres, and that this work will be fraught with difficulties.[22] Nevertheless Gaskell affirms that it is possible to create better social and private arrangements, and that the two spheres are tied together—indeed, married.

Notes

1. Williams finds Gaskell's second novel less interesting because it contains less tension. In its favor, he cites an intriguing resemblance between Margaret, a sympathetic observer, and Gaskell herself, which he says creates more successful integration in the novel (*Culture and Society, 1780-1950*, 91). On the other hand, Foster calls *North and South* a "bolder and more accomplished version of *Mary Barton*" (*Victorian Women's Fiction*, 147).

2. *North and South*, 416; hereafter page numbers are cited in parentheses in the text. Bodenheimer suggests that Margaret's struggle to define her life is "presented as a battle against forms of idleness" and observes that "how she is to spend her days is an explicit issue" in the novel (*The Politics of Story in Victorian Social Fiction*, 63).

3. Showalter rightly describes Margaret Hale as "intellectual" and "self-defining" (*A Literature of Their Own*, 122). Calder believes that Margaret is the least confined of Gaskell's heroines and that she is also the most self-aware (*Women and Marriage in Victorian Fiction*, 79). Calder also regards Gaskell's portrayal of Margaret of a general pattern in her fiction, which often deals with "women who learn, women who change through experience and crisis" (80). Basch views Margaret as worthy of her vocation of bringing about a reconciliation between the agricultural South and the industrial North "by virtue of her intelligence and her high humanitarian and religious consciousness" (*Relative Creatures*, 67).

4. Schor asserts that instead of moving toward a resolution in romance "*North and South* in fact moves in the opposite direction: from the 'romance' of the heroine's life and her progress toward marriage into the density of industrial England and its economic and sexual politics" (*Scheherezade in the Marketplace*, 120).

5. Uglow explains that Gaskell used her memories of a visit to Capesthorne to see Caroline Davenport's trousseau as material for the scene in which Edith's wedding preparations are described (*Elizabeth Gaskell*, 299).

6. Bodenheimer notes that "matrimonial calculation and fusses about weddings, dress, and status are the staples of the female realm in *North and South*; Margaret is drawn away from them, into dialogues with men and social activity" (*The Politics of Story in Victorian Social Fiction*, 63).

7. For an informative discussion of the contribution that Victorian women made in philanthropy, see Summers, "A Home from Home: Women's Philanthropic Work in the Nineteenth Century," in *Fit Work for Women*, ed. Sandra Burman, 33-63.

8. Spencer observes that Margaret is "Gaskell's most Ruskinian woman, performing a vital social work that is an extension of her personal duties" (*Elizabeth Gaskell*, 91).

9. Foster contends that Gaskell's works often examine "the possibilities of female self-assertion, with their heroines revealing surprisingly 'unfeminine' energies" (*Victorian Women's Fiction: Marriage, Freedom and the Individual*, 143).

10. Gaskell was willing for one of her daughters, Meta, to pursue nursing as a career, but remained doubtful that she would have the commitment to make that choice.

11. Cosslett, *Woman to Woman*, focuses on the importance of friendships between women in the development of female identity and discusses how this idea is played out in *Wives and Daughters*. She fails, however, to apply her thesis to *North and South*. David underestimates Bessie's significance in the novel, dismissing her as one who has an "unengaged and unengaging role" (*Fictions of Resolution in Three Victorian Novels*, 39).

12. Harman explains that Margaret's willingness to strike up an acquaintance with one of the men is "a sign of [her] increasing willingness to mix with the world and to accommodate herself to the complicated class relations that . . . life in the public realm seems to entail" ("In Promiscuous Company," 366).

13. Uglow cites biographical evidence that Gaskell had "seen numerous idealistic young women" who, like Margaret, were "excited yet disturbed by Manchester," including Annie Shaen, Charlotte Froude, and Adelaide Procter (*Elizabeth Gaskell*, 369).

14. In this scene and others, Margaret demonstrates her ability to reason, to think carefully through a complicated issue. Based on Gaskell's presentation of many of her women characters, I strongly disagree with Bonaparte, who concludes that Gaskell believes that "women have . . . no intellectual ability" and that thinking is not "a woman's task" (*The Gypsy-Bachelor of Manchester*, 36). To support her conclusion, Bonaparte gives undue weight to a casual comment about women's judgement in one of Gaskell's letters, ignoring many counter pieces of evidence.

15. Bodenheimer credits Gaskell with exploding the metaphor of social paternalism, which sees the employer as a parent and the workers as children (*The Politics of Story in Victorian Social Fiction*, 54-5).

16. Bodenheimer discerns that Margaret Hale is a heroine "whose life is responsibly and directly entangled with the male world of industrial politics" (ibid., 53-4).

17. Spencer suggests that Margaret "acts most successfully by bringing out the womanliness within men" (*Elizabeth Gaskell*, 95).

18. Lansbury, *Elizabeth Gaskell: The Novel of Social Crisis*, 112.

19. Gallagher asserts that the moral influence women exert on men is the force connecting public and private life in the novel (*The Industrial Reformation of English Fiction*, 168).

20. In *Felix Holt*, in contrast, Esther Lyon is continually instructed by Felix Holt.

21. Harman has offered an interesting reading of this scene, claiming that it makes visible the rivalry between Margaret and John Thornton and prompts some unresolved questions: "Who shall take command? Who shall protect whom? Who shall speak? Who shall act? Who shall really 'appear'?" ("In Promiscuous Company," 367).

22. Bodenheimer argues that Gaskell negotiates the political and the private realm in her romantic solution by defining it as "an economic and social partnership as well as a domestic settlement" (*The Politics of Story in Victorian Social Fiction*, 63). Foster sees the same connection between the personal and the public realm and affirms that female power, "centered in the responses of the heart, is the real revolutionary force" uncovered by the novel (*Victorian Women's Fiction*, 148).

Chapter 5

Among the Amazons: *Cranford*

Cranford (1851) is an often-misunderstood work which Gaskell wrote between *Mary Barton* and *North and South*. Because the two industrial novels address many of the same issues, I have discussed them sequentially. However, the historical chronology of these works is revealing, for it suggests that Gaskell moved easily from an examination of public problems in the market economy to one of private problems in a small country village, and back again. Gaskell's ease in navigating between these two seemingly disconnected worlds indicates the extent to which they are connected in her own mind and works. Despite the distinction many critics have made between the genres of the industrial novel and the idyll, Gaskell certainly made no such distinction in her own mind. I wish to show that *Cranford* has more in common with the so-called "industrial novels" than has been recognized. Of particular importance in the novel is Gaskell's success in collapsing the public and private spheres.

Cranford (1851) has been dismissed by many as a quaint period piece about life in a small English village. Quite popular throughout the nineteenth century, *Cranford* was well known and loved by readers, many of whom could recite whole passages from the novel. Because *Cranford* does not overtly grapple with the social problems which form the subject matter of some of Gaskell's more respected novels, it has been wrongly characterized as presenting a kind of rose-colored picture of life. Readers who come to the work with such an impression might be surprised to find within its supposedly idyllic pages the realities of romantic disappointment, family estrangement, crime, financial ruin, and death. In this work problems of the public sphere, especially the problems of women, are embedded within private events. However, Gaskell's apparent shift in focus from the industrial mode, which foregrounds social issues, to the domestic mode, signals not an abandonment of the public world, but a more intensive engagement with its problems, which she comes to see as inscribed within the private sphere.

In *Cranford*, Gaskell returns to a literary mode which had interested her at the beginning of her career when she and her husband planned to write together a series of poetic "Sketches Among the Poor."[1] Although only one of these scenes from Manchester life was ever finished, Gaskell retained an interest in observing and recording the changing social scene all around her. *Cranford* evokes the nostalgic, idyllic tone which had been popular in the days of Gaskell's youth. In particular, *Cranford* is reminiscent of the series of sketches by Mary Russell Mitford, called *Our Village* (1824).

Both Mitford and Gaskell celebrate rural life and rural people, yet their emphases are quite different. In *Our Village*, Mitford pays tribute to ordinary folk, like a competent dairywoman, a famous cricket player, and the local doctor. However, Mitford's sketches rarely go beyond description into social criticism: a typical instance of her method is her treatment of a country boy named Joe Kirby, whose "patched round frock, and the ragged condition of those unpatched shoes," never seem to trouble Mitford. Indeed, she asks, "Why should I lament the poverty that never troubles him?" and assures the reader that "Joe is the merriest and happiest creature that ever lived twelve years in this wicked world."[2] Moreover, Mitford is generally content to evoke and linger over the beauties of the English countryside, making an event out of a hunt for violets, the sight of the first primrose, the falling of the leaves. Compared to Gaskell, Mitford is more likely to focus on the natural world than on the social scene and to take male figures as her subjects, as well as less likely to examine closely the lives and problems of women.

Although she too affirms the rural world, Gaskell attempts in *Cranford* to do much more than Mitford did in *Our Village*. Interestingly, *Cranford* has particular significance for Gaskell herself: out of all of her novels, she named *Cranford* as her favorite, the one she could return to with pleasure again and again. Gaskell's fondness for this novel is telling, for the world of Cranford is a world of women. The opening lines establish Cranford as a female domain: "In the first place, Cranford is in possession of the Amazons."[3] Men are conspicuously absent: "Whatever does become of the gentlemen, they are not at Cranford. What could they do if they were there?" (1) For everything from keeping the gardens to settling questions about literature or politics, the ladies of Cranford are, Gaskell says, "quite sufficient" (2). The opening pages describe what has been described as a kind of female utopia, in which women hold sway and men are kept at bay.[4] However, Gaskell was more of a practical reformer than a utopian thinker. While she believed that society could be improved, she was no dreamy visionary. In *Cranford* Gaskell offers a social model which operates under values which run counter to those of the capitalist patriarchy.

Not all critics have regarded the novel as a positive treatment of aging women.[5] Yet such readings of *Cranford* overlook the strengths of the deceptively gentle ladies. Elizabeth Gaskell in this novel is slyly presenting ideas about social reform. Although Cranford is not a perfect society, Gaskell concentrates on the ways in which the elderly ladies manage, despite crises and disappointments, to sustain their self-made community.[6] To make a community is, of course, a political act: it is a way of consolidating power for the uses of its members. By organizing and defining themselves within a community, the Cranford ladies create an environment which serves their needs and interests. It is interesting to recall that the first Women's Rights Convention in Seneca Falls had been held only three years before *Cranford* was published. We may read this seemingly innocuous novel as Gaskell's contribution to the "Woman Question."

In her depiction of the Cranfordians, Gaskell presents an alternative to the set of social practices associated with middle-class women. In contrast to the material displays which their middle-class counterparts aspire to, the inhabitants of Cranford practice "elegant economy," keeping early hours, serving simple refreshments at entertainments, and dressing simply. Faced with limited incomes, the ladies have learned to be resourceful and to redefine gentility by dissociating it with money. This new way of looking at social success is ultimately liberating, for if money is not a prerequisite to manners, the circle widens. Displaying a "kindly *esprit de corps*," the Cranfordians "overlook all deficiencies in success when some among them tried to conceal their poverty" (4). When, for instance, Mrs. Forrester gives a party and her servant asked the guests on the sofa if she could get out the tea tray from underneath, "every one took this novel proceeding as the most natural thing in the world" (4). Further, the hostess works side by side with her servant, tending to the cakes, while, all along, the narrator says, "she knew, and we knew, and she knew that we knew" (4). Modifying social practices rituals allows the women to support each other as together they face economic necessity with dignity. Again, as she did in *Mary Barton*, Gaskell is emphasizing feminine cooperation rather than competition between members of groups.

The inhabitants of Cranford not only face the challenge of poverty, but they also experience the difficulties of living without men. Interestingly, the 1851 Census confirmed the social trend that Gaskell represents in *Cranford*, published the same year. No less than 42 percent of women between the ages of twenty and forty were unmarried, and two million--a third of Britain's population--supported themselves. The cultural expectation that women will marry and be supported by men was not being borne out by the experience of an increasingly large group of women. Within this changing landscape, Gaskell implies, women need to develop their own strategies as they try to lead useful, satisfying lives. Given the statistical reality that women had to live with, Gaskell regards the ideology of feminine leisure as not just irrelevant, but as positively dangerous.

As the Victorian feminists knew--and as Gaskell knew--there is power in numbers. Herself a member of a network of writers and activists, Gaskell approved of female solidarity and made it a major theme in her fiction. In *Cranford*, women have learned to depend on each other, particularly in a crisis. On one occasion the ladies deal with the possibility of robbery after several thefts break out in their town.[7] It is true that the ladies become frightened; indeed, they bolt themselves up when fear hits them, but when it passes, they "recollected [them]selves and set out afresh with double valiance" (135). Their impulse here is sound: they band together to weather a crisis. Alarmed at strangers passing near her house, Miss Pole hurries over to Miss Matty's house and asks for permission to spend the night: "I am come to throw myself on your hospitality" (138). Her servant Betty likewise seeks the safety of female company as she makes plans to stay with her cousin. And when a more immediate crisis surfaces, the discovery that Signor Brunoni is ill and in financial need, the ladies put their fears for their own safety aside and begin to provide assistance to the Brunoni family. Miss Matty takes the lead by sending the sedan-chair for him, Lady Glenmire presides over the medicine, Mrs. Forrester makes some bread-jelly, and Miss Pole comes and goes with her basket at all hours, by way of an unfrequented road. As Lansbury has pointed out, the ladies of Cranford know how to respond to emergencies, whether they affect the community at large or individual members.[8]

Critics who see Cranford as stagnant and insular fail to take into account the changes which occur in the town throughout the novel. Thus the characterization of Cranford society as excessively inflexible and excessively preoccupied with decorum is completely inaccurate, for Miss Matty exercises a liberating influence on her community, leading them as they gradually adopt freer attitudes toward men and class distinctions.[9] As she depicts these changes, Gaskell is suggesting that the leadership of women will lead to more flexible and humane social arrangements. When Miss Matty receives an invitation to dine with her old beau, she is at first reluctant to go, feeling that it would be improper. Yet she overcomes her misgivings and accepts the invitation. The occasion proves harmless and even enjoyable: with still a trace of guilt, Miss Matty says afterwards, "It is very pleasant dining with a bachelor . . . . I only hope it is not improper; so many pleasant things are!" (50). After this encounter with her old love, Miss Matty amends her previous stance forbidding her servant Martha to receive callers, saying "God forbid that I should grieve any young hearts" (60). Equally important, Miss Matty serves as a social mediator when Mrs. Jamieson's behavior strains social relations in Cranford and she persuades her neighbors to accept the socially unequal marriage of Mr. Hoggins and Lady Glenmire. Miss Matty thus functions as a progressive leader of her community, calling for changes which will enhance the lives of the inhabitants of Cranford.

Gaskell allows economic realities to enter the plot of *Cranford* in order to illustrate the precarious situation of women who are not trained to be self-supporting; here Gaskell is drawing attention to the plight of unskilled women who cannot rely on either husbands or families for financial support. At the same time, she wants to confer on her characters a kind of resilience which will help them to improvise, to create space for themselves within the working world.

One of the most significant events in the novel occurs when the Town and Country Bank fails, causing Miss Matty to lose a large portion of her income. Miss Matty exhibits remarkable courage and strength when faced with the possibility of financial ruin. Shopping for a new silk, Miss Matty overhears the shopman reject a neighbor's five-pound note. With the "soft dignified manner peculiar to her . . . which became her so well," Miss Matty takes action in this situation, offering the man five sovereigns for his note because, as a shareholder, she sees herself as responsible for the protection of her community (187-8). After returning home, Miss Matty begins to assess her circumstances and determine what she will do. When a look at her account book reveals that she will be left with only thirteen pounds a year, Miss Matty becomes despondent, but after tea, the narrator says, "We took to our work," indicating that in this case, as in others, the Cranford ladies work together to handle difficulties (193). The young narrator, Mary Smith, says, "It was an example to me...to see how immediately Miss Matty set about the retrenchment which she knew to be right under her altered circumstances" (195). Hilary Schor notes Mary Smith's development in the novel, suggesting that "she moves from anonymous reporter to amused reader and finally to manipulator/and fairy godmother."[10] I would suggest that Miss Matty deserves some of the credit for Mary Smith's development as she teaches the young girl how to marshal limited resources and how to respond to a crisis. First Miss Matty asks Mary Smith to write her father and ask him to come for a consultation, and then she determines to fit up a single room to live in and to sell the rest of her furniture. Both actions require fortitude, for, according to the unspoken code of Cranford, money matters should not be discussed with friends, much less with outsiders; furthermore, Miss Matty is fondly attached to her home, and to part with her few possessions grieves her deeply.

Miss Matty's community also assists her as she takes steps toward active employment. Gaskell's letters reveal repeated instances in which she intervened in the life of a woman who was in some kind of need. Thus, this portion of the novel records Gaskell's endorsement of a feminine network in which members respond sensitively and immediately to other women. Having discussed Miss Mattie's situation privately, the ladies of Cranford determine each to contribute a portion to assist her. The whole business is transacted discreetly, every lady writing down the sum she could give annually, signing the paper, and sealing it. This proceeding preserves the dignity of the participants, as well as the one in need. Similarly, Miss Matty's loyal servant, Martha, hastens her own wedding plans in order to offer her mistress a room as a lodger in her new home. As Gaskell creates these scenes, she emphasizes the communal values which sustain the women in Cranford and demonstrates how they work together to survive all sorts of crises.

Cranford dramatizes the dilemma faced by women who are compelled to find work but who have not had the chance to develop the skills that are rewarded in the marketplace. At the same time, it affirms the resourcefulness and creativity that women can discover in themselves when given the opportunity. Mary Smith displays this resourcefulness when she comes up with the idea that Miss Matty could support herself by selling tea.[11] Mary Smith "thought of all the things by which a woman, past middle age, and with the education common to ladies fifty years ago, could earn or add to a living without materially losing caste" (198-9). Teaching was "of course, the first thing that suggested itself" (199). But after a mental survey of Miss Matty's accomplishments, Mary realizes that her friend lacks the skills which would be necessary to a teacher: music, drawing, sewing, reading, writing, and arithmetic—in all of these Miss Matty was deficient. What she excelled at—making candle lighters and decorating playing cards—was of no real value in the marketplace. Mary Smith is forced to conclude that "there was nothing that she could teach to the rising generation of Cranford" (201). This situation tests Mary Smith's ingenuity; urgently seeking a possible solution to Miss Matty's problem, the narrator says that when the tea was brought in an idea came into her head: "Why should not Miss Matty sell tea—be an agent to the East India Tea Company?" (202).[12] In this episode Gaskell displays an awareness of the economic realities which make it necessary for women to find work. At the same time, Gaskell demonstrates that they *can be* self-supporting. By suggesting that in this case it is Miss Matty's experience with household management which prepares her to run a successful business, Gaskell is pointing out to women that their domestic work skills can be mobilized in more public work settings.

Despite the odds against her, Miss Matty proves herself equal to the challenge before her. Her initial reaction to the plan, however, is to express self-doubt:

> It was rather a shock to her; not on account of any personal loss of gentility involved, but only because she distrusted her own powers of action in a new line of life, and would timidly have preferred a little more privation to any exertion for which she feared she was unfitted. (217)

These are the kinds of doubts which are instilled by a social ideology that officially segregates women out of the public, productive sector of the economy. Yet with the encouragement of Mary Smith and her father, who heartily approves of his daughter's scheme, Miss Matty agrees to the preparations for the new business venture. It is not true, as Martin Dodsworth has claimed, that only Miss Matty's "patience and her acceptance of straitened circumstances" are required in this situation.[13] Against her upbringing, Miss Matty has to accept the idea of participating in trade, and, perhaps more difficult, she has to allow her home to be rearranged to serve as a site for business. The dining parlour is converted into a shop, with a table serving as a counter and one window being changed into a glass door. Miss Matty is flexible enough to accommodate herself to her new situation. After the room has been cleaned and arranged, she and Mary Smith actually feel pride as they look around themselves on the evening before the shop is to be opened. In this scene Gaskell conveys her approval of her character's bravery in taking on such a project, especially given her advanced age and social conditioning.

Miss Matty's business venture not only provides an example of female enterprise, but also provides a new paradigm for the commercial ethos. When newly empowered merchants like Miss Matty enter the workplace, Gaskell implies that the strictly competitive structure of business will be infused with the womanly values of cooperation and mutual support. For instance, Miss Matty is reluctant to sell tea while Mr. Johnson, a neighbor, includes the item in his shop; consequently, she confides to him her plans and inquires whether they are likely to injure his business. Although Mary Smith's father calls this idea of hers "great nonsense," questioning how tradespeople "were to get on if there was to be a continual consulting of each others' interests," her action ultimately serves her own interests, for Mr. Johnson subsequently sends customers to her, claiming that Miss Jenkyns had the really choice teas (220). As Elizabeth Langland has noted, Miss Matty actually "establishes an edge over her competitor by telling him that she will not compete."[14] Likewise, Miss Matty's way of dealing with unfair practices is effective and constructive. When the man who brings her coal shortchanges her, she says quietly, "I am sure you would be sorry to bring me wrong weight," therefore putting a stop to his dishonest treatment of her (221). Thus chided by a trusting old woman, the man is ashamed to cheat her again. In contrast, Mary's father, who is skeptical of Miss Matty's methods, admits that he lost more than a thousand pounds the previous year, despite all his precautions. The more Miss Matty gives away, the more she is rewarded: gifts of a few eggs, fresh ripe fruit, a bunch of flowers regularly appear on her counter. Gaskell seems hopeful about the possibility of women imbuing the capitalist system with a feminine ethos, or, as Nina Auerbach puts it, of investing "laissez-faire reality with [their] communality."[15] Miss Matty is successful in her business; the first year she makes more than twenty pounds, and she actually comes to enjoy the employment, "which brought her into kindly intercourse with many of the people around her" (226).

Gaskell's vision of a community of women transcends individual self-sufficiency.[16] As a minister's wife in the urban district of Manchester, Gaskell's eyes were opened to social problems; hence, her novels regularly contain implications about the future of society as a whole. As a female novelist, she knew of the value of community, identifying herself with a group of women writers and willingly using her own position to help other women.

Jenny Uglow describes Gaskell's feminist circle, a circle which included "older mentors" like Harriet Martineau, Mary Howitt, and Anna Jameson, as well as younger activists like Bessie Parkes, Barbara Leigh Smith, Adelaide Proctor, Anna Mary Howitt, and Miranda and Octavia Hill.[17]   In this seeming innocuous novel, Gaskell reveals how a group of elderly women can sustain and sensitize their community and, furthermore, how a nurturing community can bring out the latent strengths of its individual members. Pauline Nestor has said that *Cranford* shows that it is "possible to imagine a community of women without men, in which marriage is not regarded . . . as the sole . . . destiny of any woman and which has value and honour."[18]   While charting the lives of leading feminists in Victorian England, Philippa Levine has noted that feminists sought to "reconstitute a positive image of singleness as an issue of personal choice rather than an uninvited catastrophe."[19]   In her presentation of the elderly ladies of Cranford, Gaskell joins the feminist enterprise of raising the status of single women by pointing out their current predicaments and by affirming their choices about their own destinies. Like *Mary Barton* and *North and South*, *Cranford* is eminently political.

Notes

1. For a more detailed discussion of "Sketches among the Poor," see Uglow, *Elizabeth Gaskell*, 101.

2. Mitford, *Our Village*, 57.

3. *Cranford*, 1; hereafter, page numbers are cited in parentheses in the text.

4. Lansbury asserts that Cranford is "as much a Utopia as any devised by a social reformer." See *Elizabeth Gaskell*, 86.

5. Dodsworth was the first to argue that Gaskell wishes to show the "full horror" of the Cranford situation, in which the women only pretend to be sufficient without men (139). Dodsworth sees the Cranfordians as neurotic, hysterical, helpless, and repressed. See "Women Without Men at *Cranford*," *Essays in Criticism* 13 (1963): 132-45. Martin takes a similarly negative view when she calls *Cranford* a "study of trivia" (74). She believes that Gaskell's purpose is to help women realize that "they were themselves, to a large extent, to blame for the inanities of their lives" (80). See *Petticoat Rebels*. Beer calls the women of Cranford "self-deceiving frustrated spinsters" (159). See *Reader, I Married Him*. More recently, Stoneman has seen Cranford as "the result of marginalisation" (88). Stoneman is critical of Miss Matty as a heroine, citing her frequent naps, her preference for darkness, her feebleness. To Stoneman, Miss Matty is a victim of the nineteenth century's infantilization of women. See *Elizabeth Gaskell*.

6. The pattern of women sustaining other women runs through Gaskell's body of fiction. Her first published work, "Libbie Marsh's Three Eras," (1847) contains this theme of female solidarity, as does "The Well of Pen-Morfa" (1850) and "Half a Life-time ago" (1855). Williams suggests that Gaskell is interested in showing that "women can expect more kindness from each other than from men." See *Women in the English Novel*, 109.

7. Dodsworth exaggerates the degree of panic which grips the Cranford ladies while overlooking the strategies which they develop to cope in a time of danger. See "Women Without Men at *Cranford*," 141.

8. See *Elizabeth Gaskell*, 86.

9. Schor (*Scheherezade in the Marketplace*) suggests that *Cranford* "does not, strictly speaking, have a heroine: Miss Matty represents some kind of moral center for the novel"(113).

10. Ibid., 88.

11. Brodetsky notes an interesting correspondence between character and author: "Mary Smith, in her comings and goings between Cranford and Drumble, brings to mind the life of Elizabeth Gaskell herself, especially during the first years of her married life." See *Elizabeth Gaskell*, 34.

12. Schor (*Scheherezade in the Marketplace*) connects Mary Smith's increasing involvement in addressing Miss Matty's predicament and Gaskell's increasingly complex use of her as a narrator: "As she assumes narrative responsibility--telling readers more about herself, admitting her own doubts about that everyday life with her father in Drumble, becoming increasingly ironic and identified with the Cranfordian imagination--so she begins to act in the narrative: writing the letter to Miss Matty's brother, against all the male, practical discouragement she can imagine; coming up with the plan for Miss Matty's financial independence in running the tea shop; becoming more her own person, more her own heroine"(114).

13. Dodsworth, "Women Without Men at *Cranford*," 143.

14. Langland, "Nobody's Angels: Domestic Ideology and Middle-Class Women in the Victorian Novel," *PMLA* 107 (1992), 299.

15. Auerbach, *Communities of Women: An Idea in Fiction*, 86.

16. Wolfe has observed that Gaskell's portrayal of the women of Cranford concentrates on "feminine strength." Yet Wolfe overlooks the intervention of neighbors when she argues that Miss Matty is able to "stand by herself as her decisiveness in misfortune and her success in business have proven" (175). See "Structure and Movement in *Cranford*," 161-76.

17. See *Elizabeth Gaskell* for an account of the dynamics within Gaskell's widening circle of women friends (311). Auerbach emphasizes Gaskell's unconventionality as she ventures into an "uncharted world" in her delineation of "governing women whose self-definitions come from their freedom from family." See *Communities of Women: An Idea in Fiction*, 6. Davis makes the distinction between biological and social mothering and claims that in *Cranford* Gaskell envisions a "community of social mothers who do not become depleted because their lack of family and marital obligations allows them to mother each other" (528). See "Feminist Critics and Literary Mothers: Daughters Reading Elizabeth Gaskell," *Signs* 17 (1992): 507-532. Said's distinction between filiation and affiliation may also apply here. See *The World, the Text, and the Critic*, 16-20.

18. Nestor, *Female Friendships and Communities*, 56.

19. Levine, *Feminist Lives*, 45.

Chapter 6

Separate Duties—"Not Opposing Each Other; Not Impossible, But Difficult To Be Reconciled": *The Life of Charlotte Brontë*

Like *Mary Barton* and *North and South*, *The Life of Charlotte Brontë* (1857) explores the connection between the public and the private. The *Life* confronts the issue of female vocation by strategically reinterpreting the life of a woman who by committing herself to a literary vocation had become the object of public hostility because of the way she pursued that career. As a biographer and a friend, Gaskell had as her main purpose the defense of Brontë before an audience critical of what was considered her shocking fiction.[1] Aware of the value of a secure reputation, Gaskell is determined to bring Brontë, marginalized by an audience that views her as aberrant and unnatural, back into the community of women. Confronting a negative public perception, Gaskell attempts to reveal the private side of the woman in order to reconfigure Brontë's public image as a writer. Gaskell's strategy of emphasizing the womanly side of Brontë may be viewed as typical of Victorian feminists like Anna Jameson, Barbara Bodichon, and Jessie Boucherette, who, keeping their ends firmly in mind, often put their arguments in terms that would be acceptable to their culture. Yet Gaskell's work is more than an expression of friendship and support from one writer to another: in the *Life* Gaskell seeks to reform her culture's understanding of femininity by demonstrating that a woman's vocation is not incompatible with her family responsibilities. As she writes about Charlotte Brontë, Gaskell urges her culture to value the work of women done in both the private and the public domains.

Roland Barthes has called biography "a novel that dare not speak its name," while Carolyn Heilbrun has observed that "biographies are fictions, constructions by the biographer of the story she or he had to tell."[2] Gaskell's *Life of Charlotte Brontë* may rightly be viewed as a novelistic account of Charlotte Brontë motivated in part by Gaskell's need to confront her own ambiguous position as a woman/artist in the nineteenth century. In "On History" (1830) Carlyle declared that history was the "essence of innumerable biographies." The nineteenth-century fascination with biography found expression in a proliferation of memoirs, reminiscences, and even poems or novels that claimed to be accounts of an individual's life. It began early in the century with the Romantic interest in individual experience and continued through the Victorian period often in the form of hagiography.[3] While Boswell had wanted to amass as many personal, idiosyncratic details about Johnson as possible, Victorian biographers felt an obligation to protect the privacy of their subjects; as Alan Shelston has pointed out, "'Truth' was a Victorian ideal, but so too was discretion."[4] As a consequence, Victorian biographies, often written by someone who was intimate with the subject, are peculiar works that attempt to reveal and disclose at the same time. Gaskell's *Life of Charlotte Brontë* (1857) is no exception. As a close friend of Charlotte Brontë for many years, Gaskell appeared to be a safe choice for biographer. Concerned with the public perception of his daughter, Patrick Brontë commissioned Gaskell to create an account of her life that would justify her to her many critics. When approached by Brontë's father, Gaskell accepted the responsibility of writing a biography that would do justice to the memory of the vilified Miss Brontë. From the beginning Gaskell regarded the project as a sacred trust. In a letter she confides, "I was under a solemn promise to write the Life,—although I shrank from the task . . . But it did not seem to me right to shrink from the work as soon as it appeared to me in the light of a duty" (Letter 347a).

Although Gaskell was committed to writing the *Life*, she experienced a great deal of discomfort and resistance in the process of composition. On a particularly trying day, she complains, "I hate the whole affair, & every thing connected with it" (Letter 348). Inevitably, she seems to have resigned herself to the difficulties of the work: "To do it at all it was necessary to tell painful truths. Like all pieces of human life, faithfully told there must be some great lesson to be learnt" (Letter 347a).

Despite Gaskell's best efforts to be truthful, the publication of the biography occasioned even more turmoil; the whole thing became what Gaskell called a "hornet's nest with a vengeance" (Letter 352). Besides being pelted with letters charging inaccuracies, Gaskell had to face the possibility of libel lawsuits. Even worse was the pervasive sense of public disapproval that was so hard for her to bear. In a letter to Brontë's friend Ellen Nussey, Gaskell says, "I have cried more since I came home than I ever did in the same space of time before" (Letter 352). In the face of discouragement, Gaskell nevertheless clung to her conviction that she had acquitted herself of her duty: "I *did so try* to *tell the truth*, & I believe *now* I hit as near the truth as any one *could* do. And I weighed every line with all my whole power & heart, so that every line should go to its great purpose of making *her* known & valued, as one who had gone through such a terrible life with a brave & faithful heart" (Letter 352). The strong response to Gaskell's work suggests that the public myths surrounding Brontë were so firmly entrenched that any effort to correct them was vehemently rejected by an audience that preferred its own version of the truth.

Although for each of the novels she wrote, Gaskell's letters reveal glimpses of the strain of composition, writing the *Life* seems to have been particularly traumatic. Why was this work more difficult for Gaskell to write than some of her novels? In all likelihood, it was because this book, the only one of Gaskell's works that deals with woman as artist, struck at the core of Gaskell's own professional and personal identity. Françoise Basch suggests that in Charlotte Brontë, Gaskell "found her own problem of the hierarchy of duties experienced more acutely, resolved more fanatically."[5] Confronting the life of Charlotte Brontë, Gaskell was forced to examine her own. Under the cover of biography, Gaskell displaced some of her personal anxieties about her performance of womanly duties by representing Brontë as a writer for whom family always came first. Moreover, by underscoring Brontë's competence in traditionally feminine activities alongside literary accomplishments, Gaskell created the possibility of an enlarged definition of womanliness. The most challenging aspect of Gaskell's task was to remake Brontë's image, to recover her "feminine" qualities. Contemporary reviews of Brontë's novels frequently noted the "masculine tone" present, the "male mind" at work in the fiction. Furthermore, there are frequent complaints of "coarseness," of a "low tone of behaviour" that offended Victorian sensibilities.[6] As Gaskell saw it, her first obligation was to present a feminized version of Brontë, one that would make her more acceptable to her society. Carolyn Heilbrun oversimplifies when she argues that Gaskell "restored Brontë to the safety of womanliness."[7] Philippa Levine is more insightful when she presents Gaskell's strategy as consistent with that of other Victorian feminists, who were eager to characterize single women as womanly in order to restore both "humanity and womanhood to women stripped of their identity by their absence of marital status."[8] However, Gaskell intends to do more than that: her aim is to broaden her culture's conception of womanliness.

Very early in the *Life* Gaskell gives a detailed physical description of Charlotte Brontë, emphasizing her feminine qualities. Gaskell recognizes the importance of establishing an image of the writer that would appeal to Victorian readers.[9] As she describes Brontë, Gaskell dwells on those features so often attributed to fictional heroines, particularly her diminutive frame, luxurious hair, luminous eyes, and delicate hands. The primary focus of the picture Gaskell presents is Brontë's smallness. Gaskell wants her readers to see Brontë's "slight, fragile body," her physical powerlessness linking her with other women. Her hands and feet, Gaskell says, "were the smallest I ever saw; when one of the former was placed in mine, it was like the soft touch of a bird in the middle of my palm."[10] Brushing quickly over Brontë's physical defects, Gaskell creates an image of femininity.

At the same time, Gaskell allows for intellectual power in Brontë, describing her great mental and literary gifts; Gaskell makes it a point to show that

femininity and intellectual power can coexist. Along with the description of
Brontë's eyes, Gaskell mentions her usual expression of "quiet, listening
intelligence" (124). The characterization of Brontë's intelligence as quiet makes
room for her pursuit of individual interests. Gaskell even refers directly to
Brontë's literary talents, but again places these talents in a context that would
make them more acceptable to Victorian society. The reference occurs in a
comment about Brontë's delicate, long fingers, whose fineness of sensation "was
one reason why all her handiwork, of whatever kind—writing, sewing,
knitting—was so clear in its minuteness" (124). This extraordinarily sly allusion
to novel writing as "handiwork" exemplifies Gaskell's strategy as she tries to
reconcile Brontë's need to write with her identity as a Victorian woman.

Moreover, Gaskell emphasizes Brontë's scrupulousness in the performance
of traditionally "feminine" responsibilities—to her family and to her community.
Gaskell even goes so far as to portray Brontë as somewhat of a martyr, hoping
to evoke both pity and sympathy for her. By filling the *Life* with pictures of
Brontë surrounded by her family members, Gaskell attempts to call up the image
of the family circle so revered by the Victorians. Early in the biography,
Gaskell recounts the circumstances surrounding the death of the oldest, Maria,
and the effect of her death on Charlotte: "Charlotte was thus suddenly called
into the responsibilities of eldest sister in a motherless family" (109). Young
and motherless herself, Charlotte was forced to accept an adult role:
"Charlotte's deep thoughtful spirit appears to have felt almost painfully the
tender responsibility which rested upon her with reference to her remaining
sisters. She was only eighteen months older than Emily; but Emily and Anne
were simply companions and playmates, while Charlotte was motherly friend
and guardian to both; and this loving assumption of duties beyond her years,
made her feel considerably older than she really was" (111). With this
characterization of Charlotte as a motherless child, overburdened with cares and
sorrows, Gaskell links her heroine to the large company of motherless children
in Victorian novels, thus eliciting pity and sympathy for the publicly
misunderstood Brontë.

Fulfilling an adult role required attention to the tasks of running a large
household; Gaskell relates how Charlotte had "to brush rooms, to run errands,
to help in the simpler forms of cooking, to be by turns playfellow and monitress
to her younger sisters and brothers, to make and to mend, and to study economy
under her careful aunt" (121). After returning from school at Roe Head,
Charlotte was kept busy teaching her sisters, in addition to serving regularly as
a teacher at the Sunday school. Gaskell allows these details to accrue, building
a portrait of Charlotte as one who was at home and successful within the
domestic sphere. Representing Charlotte as an exemplar of domesticity enables
Gaskell to deny charges of unnaturalness and to normalize her friend.

In her presentation of the entire Brontë household, Gaskell points out the
difference in the way vocation is played out in man's life versus a woman's life.

Gaskell emphasizes that, for the Brontë sisters, attending to the family often meant deferring or suppressing their own interests to serve those of their brother, Branwell, who was regarded as the real genius among them. In the summer of 1835 the great question in the Brontë home centered upon Branwell and his future: what profession would he choose? Gaskell writes, "The sisters hardly recognized their own, or each others' powers, but they knew *his*" (153). When both Branwell's talents and inclinations pointed in the direction of art, it was determined that he would be sent to the Royal Academy.

Gaskell reveals that this family decision prompted action on the part of Charlotte. In a letter to a friend, she confides, "I am going to be a governess. This last resolution I formed myself . . . knowing well that papa would have enough to do with his limited income, should Branwell be placed at the Royal Academy, and Emily at Roe Head" (156). Despite her dislike of children, teaching seemed to Charlotte the only available way of earning a living. Throughout the *Life* Gaskell dwells on Charlotte's experiences as a governess to win the reader's sympathy and support.

The plight of the governess was the subject of many Victorian novels. Regardless of the social expectation that they would not have to work, middle-class women were often forced to enter this field where conditions were frequently appalling. Moreover, they had to compete for limited positions in an overcrowded profession. Holcombe reports that one lady received over eight hundred applications for a governess's post.[11] Such intense competition inevitably led to lower salaries. Along with long hours and low wages, the position of governess brought little prestige: subject to the demands of her mistress, the governess was sometimes expected to perform menial household labor on top of her teaching duties.

Gaskell includes selections from Charlotte's letters that reveal the kind of effect that being a governess had on her. "Weary with a day's hard work . . . I am sitting down to write . . . . Excuse me if I say nothing but nonsense, for my mind is exhausted and dispirited" (163). "My life since I saw you has passed as monotonously and unbroken as ever; nothing but teach, teach, teach, from morning till night" (164). And most bitter of all,

> I said in my last letter that Mrs— did not know me. I now begin to find she does not intend to know me; that she cares nothing about me, except to contrive how the greatest possible quantity of labour may be got out of me; and to that end she overwhelms me with oceans of needlework; yards of cambric to hem, muslin nightcaps to make, and, above all things, dolls to dress . . . . I see more clearly than I have ever done before, that a private governess has no existence, is not considered as a living rational being, except as connected with the wearisome duties she has to fulfil. (188)

Aware that others might not understand her reaction to her work, Charlotte explains, "No one but myself is aware how utterly averse my whole mind and nature are for the employment" (212).

While she credits Charlotte for her courageous acceptance of uninspiring work ("Brave heart, ready to die in harness!"), Gaskell nevertheless regrets wasted feminine potential (182). The *Life* offers, then, both tribute and protest: tribute to the courage of a woman who steadily threw her energies into labor that was uncongenial to her and protest that a woman's gifts should be so devalued. Gaskell expresses this ambivalence toward Charlotte's life by contrasting the spoiled, indolent brother with the self-sacrificing, industrious sister.

From the beginning Gaskell emphasizes the similarities between Branwell and Charlotte, in appearance and in artistic inclination. Gaskell first points out a physical likeness: "He and his sister Charlotte were both slight and small of stature" (197). There was a mental connection as well, which led naturally enough to their collaboration on the tales, poems, and romances that were their primary means of artistic expression in childhood. Both Branwell and Charlotte showed promise early in drawing and in writing. However, since Branwell was the only boy in the family, his talents were nourished, while Charlotte's were set aside whenever domestic matters arose. Gaskell comments on the trials of the only boy in a family of girls: "He is expected to act a part in life; to *do*, while they are only to *be*" (197). On the surface Gaskell seems to be sympathizing with the son, but she is subtly suggesting that it is equally a trial to the daughter who has talents and ambitions to be expected only to *be*.

Gaskell also highlights the differences between Branwell and Charlotte by describing how they occupied themselves. In 1840 Branwell "was living at home, employing himself in occasional composition of various kinds, and waiting till some employment, for which he might be fitted without any expensive course of preliminary education, should turn up" (198). On the other hand, after all the household had gone to bed, the Brontë sisters were "free to pace up and down (like restless wild animals) in the parlour, talking over plans and projects, and thoughts of what was to be their future life" (199). The plan that seemed to be most promising to them was that of keeping a school, and "in the evenings of this winter of 1839-40, the alterations that would be necessary in the house, and the best way of convincing their aunt of the wisdom of their project, formed the principal subject of their conversation" (200). In addition, in her leisure hours that winter, Charlotte was at work on writing a story. Gaskell clearly juxtaposes the young man's passivity, his nonchalant attitude that something would come along, and the young women's active participation in their own destinies. In so doing, Gaskell makes a case for the need to take female potential and vocation seriously: despite high hopes for his success, Branwell brought only disgrace on his family, while Charlotte, despite much discouragement, managed to attain a place for herself as a novelist. Drawing a lesson from the life of Branwell, Gaskell writes, "He was to die at the end of a short and blighted life . . . . These were not the first sisters who have laid their lives as a sacrifice before their brother's idolized wish. Would to God they might be the last" (156). With so many competing obligations, Gaskell's readers might well wonder when Brontë ever found the time for reading and for writing. Gaskell takes great pains to demonstrate that womanly duties and obligations always came first for Brontë. Gaskell uses one domestic incident to clarify Brontë's priorities. When Tabby, the old housekeeper who had lived with the Brontës for many years, reached the age of eighty, she began losing her sight. However, the proud old woman refused to acknowledge her diminishing powers and refused to let the new servant assume what she considered to be her exclusive work: the job of peeling potatoes for dinner. When Tabby's failing eyesight kept her from realizing that she had left black specks in the potatoes, Brontë, a fastidious housekeeper, quietly removed the bowl of vegetables, cut out the specks, and then returned them to the kitchen. This—even in the middle of writing—Brontë would do to satisfy the imperatives of duty.

It is not likely that Gaskell felt the need to peel the potatoes herself. In fact, it was largely due to her skill in delegating work to her servants and her daughters that she was able to steal time for writing. Nevertheless she was ready to commend Charlotte Brontë for scrupulously adhering to her own strong sense of duty: "Never was the claim of any duty, never was the call of another for help, neglected for an instant" (306). In so doing, Gaskell was not primarily interested in food preparation. Rather, she was attempting to salvage the possibility of *both* domestic and literary activity for women: she was trying to show that it was possible to be both a woman and a writer.

An example will illustrate Gaskell's vision of satisfying both the domestic and the artistic realms. In a description of the Brontë kitchen, Gaskell notes that it was Emily who made all the bread for the household. Of course, in a large Victorian family, bread-making was a continuous, omnipresent activity. While attending to this mundane chore, Emily studied German out of an open book propped up in front of her, kneading the dough all the while. Gaskell wryly comments that "no study, however interesting, interfered with the goodness of the bread, which was always light and excellent" (159). She goes on to say that books were a common sight in the Brontë kitchen since the girls were "taught by their father theoretically, and by their aunt practically, that to take an active part in all household work was, in their position, woman's simple duty" (159). At the same time, Gaskell says, the Brontës "found many an odd five minutes for reading while watching the cakes, and managed the union of two kinds of employment better than King Alfred" (159). This reference to baking/reading, like the handiwork/writing analogy, sanctions women in both activities. At the same time, Gaskell implicitly acknowledges the injustice of this sense of dual responsibility, which inevitably exacted a high price for women. If we compare the number of works written by women writers like the Brontës and Eliot to the number written by Dickens, for example, it is clear that the lack of time to write was a serious problem for women.

Once Charlotte began publishing her novels, Gaskell says, her life "becomes divided into two parallel currents—her life as Currer Bell, the author; her life as Charlotte Brontë, the woman" (234). With each of these roles came separate duties, "not impossible, but difficult to be reconciled" (234). Gaskell observes that male authors are not faced with this dichotomy: "When a man becomes an author, it is probably merely a change of employment to him" (234). A woman, on the other hand, cannot "drop the domestic charges devolving on her as an individual, for the exercise of the most splendid talents that were ever bestowed" (234). However, this dilemma does not, Gaskell insists, absolve a woman from using her gifts: "And yet she must not shrink from the extra responsibility implied by the very face of her possessing such talents. She must not hide her gift in a napkin; it was meant for the use and service of others. In an humble and faithful spirit must she labour to do what is not impossible, or God would not have set her to do it" (334).

Using Charlotte Brontë's life as evidence, Gaskell affirms that a gifted woman can perform her work and discharge her family duties satisfactorily. Gaskell was capable of observing and articulating the fact that women writers lived under greater stress than male writers did, with multiple sets of obligations. However, she is so intent on presenting an acceptably feminine image of Brontë that she stops short of insisting that women writers need to be relatively free of domestic labor. At the same time, a reading of Gaskell's letters reveals a woman who created domestic arrangements that allowed her to write; capitalizing on the public/private distinction in Victorian culture, Gaskell presented an acceptable face toward the public as a dutiful wife and mother while she took the necessary liberties within her home in order to fulfill her literary (public) vocation.

In dealing with the problems suggested by Brontë's marriage, Gaskell does not attempt to suppress a certain ambivalence. In the *Life* Gaskell's aim is to present Charlotte Brontë as a "normal" woman, in short, to vindicate her before the public. Brontë's midlife marriage was, for Gaskell, an indispensable part of her story. It would, more than anything else, normalize Brontë and elicit a sympathetic response from readers.

As she does with other topics throughout the biography, Gaskell takes an ambiguous stance toward Brontë's marriage. For the most part she follows her usual pattern of drawing on excerpts from Brontë's letters, believing that she can do most service to her friend by letting her speak for herself. But Gaskell's hand is evident in the selection of particular bits of correspondence, as well as in the commentary around the letters.

When she first mentions Brontë's marriage, Gaskell displays an awareness of the difficulty of discussing the issue. This no doubt springs partly from Victorian reticence about personal matters, but also from her own conflicting responses to her friend's marital state. Indeed, Gaskell confesses, "it requires delicate handling on my part" (490).

Again to inspire admiration and pity for Brontë, Gaskell includes descriptions of the circumstances leading up to the marriage. She feels impelled first of all to establish Mr. Nicholls as an honorable man who had loved Charlotte for a long time; she insists that "he was not a man to be attracted by any kind of literary fame" (490). By portraying Nicholls as a virtuous man, Gaskell is suggesting that he recognized similarly noble qualities in Charlotte: "The love of such a man—a daily spectator of her manner of life for years—is a great testimony to her character as a woman" (490). Second, Gaskell creates interest in and support for the couple by painting them as persecuted lovers. Upon receiving a proposal, Charlotte immediately told her father, who "could not bear the idea of this attachment of Mr. Nicholls to his daughter" (491). Charlotte, always obedient, promised to comply. Gaskell comments, "Thus quietly and modestly did she, on whom such hard judgments had been passed by ignorant reviewers, receive this vehement, passionate declaration of love,—thus thoughtfully for her father, and unselfishly for herself, put aside all consideration of how she should reply, excepting as he wished!" (491). Gradually, Brontë's patience won out, as her father's opposition to the marriage lifted.

As the wife of a minister, Gaskell knew about the demands that would be placed on Charlotte and the obstructions that wifely obligations would impose between Charlotte and her writing. It is not surprising, therefore, that Gaskell's account of Charlotte's marriage, though ostensibly celebratory, reveals doubts and ominous forebodings. Never one to sentimentalize marriage, Gaskell gradually discloses the kinds of limitations that marriage placed on Brontë.

In the portions of the letters selected by Gaskell, Charlotte's references to her upcoming wedding do not sound enthusiastic; on the contrary, she seems to have had genuine misgivings about what she was planning to do. This uncertainty emerges in her language, which is sprinkled with expressions like "seems," "I hope," and "I trust" (515). Far from an enthusiastic bride, Charlotte is reserved, and does not express great expectations about her new life: "I think from Mr. Nicholls' character I may depend on this not being a mere transitory impulsive feeling, but rather that it will be accepted steadily as a duty." And later, "The destiny which Providence in His goodness and wisdom seems to offer me will not, I am aware, be generally regarded as brilliant, but I trust I see in it some germs of real happiness." About the wedding date, she mentions that "it is Mr. Nicholls' wish that the marriage should take place this summer; he urges the month of July, but that seems very soon" (515). Capturing Charlotte's hesitant, regretful attitude, Gaskell writes, "There was a strange, half-sad feeling, in making announcements of an engagement—for cares and fears came mingled inextricably with hopes" (516).

About Arthur Nicholls himself, Gaskell quotes similarly ambiguous remarks. In one letter, Charlotte characterizes her husband as a "kind, considerate fellow," who, despite his "masculine faults," "enters into my wishes" (518). On their wedding tour, the couple visited Mr. Nicholls' relatives and friends; these visits prompted Charlotte to say, "My dear husband . . . appears in a new light in his own country. More than once I have had deep pleasure in hearing his praises on all sides" (519). Charlotte probably did respect and admire her husband, but to hear continual applause for another was no doubt trying to one who had received so little of it herself. When some of the servants told her that she was fortunate to have married one of the best gentlemen in the country, Charlotte muses, "I trust I feel thankful to God for having enabled me to make what seems a right choice; and I pray to be enabled to repay as I ought the affectionate devotion of a truthful, honourable man" (519). Again, the language is tenuous, the conviction forced. Charlotte evidently sensed from the beginning that marriage would bring its own set of problems, and Gaskell captures her friend's uneasiness about her acceptance of the wifely role.

Gaskell faced a real dilemma in her treatment of Charlotte's marriage: on the one hand, she wanted to paint the pleasing image of Charlotte as fulfilled wife; on the other hand, she was forced to tell the truth as she saw it. In short, Gaskell was in the position of having to put the best public face on the matter and of honestly acknowledging the undeniable complexities of a Victorian marriage.

Thus, Gaskell's few direct remarks about Charlotte's marriage had to be equivocal. Prefacing her selections from Charlotte's letters, Gaskell recognizes the limitations an observer faces when judging another's married life: "We, her loving friends, standing outside, caught occasional glimpses of brightness, and pleasant peaceful murmurs of sound" (519). This statement serves as a disclaimer of sorts; it indicates Gaskell's unwillingness to pronounce absolutely on her friend's private life. Using similar phrasing, later Gaskell refers to Charlotte's accounts of her marriage as "the low murmurs of happiness" (520). Yet following this innocuous introduction are resigned expressions of dissatisfaction and disappointment: "I really seem to have had scarcely a spare moment since that dim quiet June morning, when you, E—, and myself all walked down to Haworth Church. Not that I have been wearied or oppressed: but the fact is, my time is not my own now; somebody else wants a good portion of it, and says, "we must do so and so." We *do* so and so accordingly; and it generally seems the right thing" (520). And on a similar note, "My own life is more occupied than it used to be: I have not so much time for thinking: I am obliged to be more practical, for my dear Arthur is a very practical, as well as a very punctual and methodical man . . . . Of course, he often finds a little work for his wife to do, and I hope she is not sorry to help him . . . . My life is different from what it used to be. May God make me thankful for it!" (521). These passages are not what one would expect from a gloriously satisfied woman; the language hints at Brontë's efforts to be content. As a writer, Gaskell is doubtless aware of the undertones that run throughout Brontë's accounts of her own marriage; this awareness produces a problem for the biographer who wants to be both faithful to the truth and to represent her friend as enjoying and succeeding in domesticity. Following Brontë herself, Gaskell employs language that is elusive and suggestive. Gaskell's repeated use of the word "murmur," for example, allows her to convey subtly her own doubts about her friend's marriage. The word carries the sense of a half-suppressed complaint. In her representation of Charlotte's marriage, Gaskell indirectly criticizes the social expectation that the wife's work will be subordinated to the husband's.

As Coral Lansbury has pointed out, "Gaskell never idealised marriage, and never saw it as more than a working partnership between individuals."[12] A look at Gaskell's own marriage is instructive here, for it sheds light on her view of the marital relationship. Winifred Gérin objects to critics who question Gaskell's satisfaction in her marriage, arguing that there is "no trace in her many allusions to [her husband] of any fundamental disharmony."[13] Apparently, Gaskell and her husband were quite different in temperament, but at the same time they shared a common set of values, both being committed to their family and to their individual work. Theirs was a sophisticated and strangely modern marriage, a marriage in which each had ample space to pursue a personal calling. Moreover, William Gaskell supported his wife to a surprising extent, given the Victorian assumption that the wife would assist the husband, rather than the other way around. Lansbury notes that William corrected his wife's proofs, helped her collect material for her *Life*, and never questioned her right to express opinions that conflicted with his own; in short, William Gaskell refused to play the role of the Victorian husband.[14] No more did Elizabeth Gaskell play the role of Victorian wife. Partly because she was fortunate in her choice of a supportive mate, Gaskell was able to write. She was sadly aware, however, that not all women were in the same position.

I have claimed that the *Life* is both tribute and protest. Barbara Weiss affirms that Gaskell, like her Victorian contemporaries, would have regarded the most important functions of literature to be inspiration and warning.[15] As she sets out to honor Charlotte Brontë, Gaskell is also covertly defending all women who, despite serious social obstacles, endeavor to pursue their vocation. She is at the same time criticizing the social conditions under which a woman writer is subjected to pressures that male writers never have to contend with. In addition, she is suggesting the need for careful choice in marriage: for a Victorian woman, the selection of an authoritarian husband could mean the indefinite postponement of any ambitions she might have.

Elaine Showalter asserts that because they were "susceptible to the self-doubt engendered by the feminine ideal, most Victorian women writers conspicuously repudiated the feminist movement even though they were basically sympathetic to its aims."[16] Gaskell did no such thing: friends with a number of the leading feminists of the day, she frequently assisted them in their projects, supporting the establishment of public nurseries and legal reforms such as the Married

Women's Property Act. On one occasion she declared to her publisher, "I think I will go in for Women's Rights" (Letter 438). Yet as a writer, she realized the importance of a public image and consequently used her position as a minister's wife and a mother to speak for all women. Pauline Nestor suggests that Gaskell's letters reveal a woman who identified herself as part of a community of women writers and concludes that she was willing to use her position to support other women writers.[17] *The Life of Charlotte Brontë* is, along with Gaskell's other works, a text that champions rights for women, particularly the right to work in the public sphere.

In a number of subtle ways, the *Life* is a daring book. It might seem, on first glance, to be a conventional treatment of women's roles within Victorian society. It does, above all, try to cast Charlotte Brontë as a woman, not a bizarre anomaly. Embedded within it, however, is an attack on a social order that hypocritically prefers women to be inactive and decorative, and does not value the work they actually do.

Contemporary response to the *Life* suggests that Gaskell succeeded in what she set out to do. The biography met with substantial critical acclaim and went through three editions. Those who attacked the book did so not on the basis of its presentation of Charlotte Brontë, but of factual inaccuracies, omissions, and the like. The many letters Gaskell received in praise of Charlotte Brontë following the publication of the *Life* attest to Gaskell's effectiveness in rehabilitating her friend's reputation.

Long before Gaskell agreed to write Charlotte Brontë's biography, she had expressed great admiration for another famous woman of her age, Florence Nightingale, who at age twenty-five announced her intention to be a nurse. Risking both social disapproval and the anger of her family, Nightingale pursued her vocation, working to improve hospital conditions in England and in the process opening up a new profession for women. In a letter expressing support of Nightingale, Gaskell refers to the role Parthe Nightingale played in furthering her sister's career: "To set F. at liberty to do her great work, Parthe has annihilated herself, her own tastes, her own wishes in order to take up all the little duties of home, to parents, to poor, to society, to servants—all the small things that fritter away time and life, *all* these Parthe does, for fear if anything was neglected people might blame F. as well as from feeling these duties imperative as if they were grand things" (Letter 217). These remarks make it clear that Gaskell knows all about the tyranny of the domestic realm, how it will fritter away both "time and life," but that she does not herself regard it as a "grand" thing. Yet it is there, and it must be managed. In a letter to her friend Eliza Fox, Gaskell refers to this conflict between "home duties" and vocation as "just my puzzle" and says, in a moment of discouragement, "I don't think I can get nearer to a solution than you have done" (Letter 68).[18]

The *Life* does not present a specific blueprint for social reform. It does, however, speak powerfully for women by affirming their gifts. Throughout her career, Gaskell spoke out for other women; it was part of her work to legitimize the work of her friends and daughters.[19]

Notes

1. I agree with Bonaparte's assertion that "What really inspired [Gaskell] to the project was that in this woman artist she saw a reflection of herself" and that "Brontë was actually in her life living the conflict in Gaskell's mind" (*The Gypsy-Bachelor of Manchester*, 232). From this point on, however, our readings of the *Life* diverge. Bonaparte believes that Gaskell denied the artist in Brontë in order to elevate the woman, while I believe that she elevated the woman in order to rescue the artist. Bonaparte concludes that Gaskell "turned *The Life of Charlotte Brontë* into the tomb of Currer Bell" (253).

2. Heilbrun, *Writing a Woman's Life*, 28.

3. Cf. the biographies of Thomas Arnold by his admiring pupil, Arthur Stanley, and the biography of Charles Kingsley by his widow.

4. Shelston, *Biography*, 9.

5. Basch, *Relative Creatures*, 46.

6. See reviews in *The Economist* 5, no. 222 (November 1847): 1376; *Graham's Magazine* 32, no. 5 (May 1848): 299; *The North American Review* 67, no. 151 (October 1848): 355-57; *The Examiner* no. 2078 (November 1847): 756-57; and *The Spectator* 21, no. 1010 (November 1847): 1074-75.

7. Heilbrun speaks in a deprecating way about Gaskell's aim and achievement, complaining that she did not "celebrate Charlotte Brontë's genius, but rescued her from the stigma of being a famous female writer, an eccentric" (*Writing a Woman's Life*, 22). I will argue that the two are, for a Victorian audience, inextricable. Other critics display their discomfort with the *Life* by omitting it from their discussions. See, for example, Davis, "Feminist Critics and Literary Mothers"; Auerbach, *Communities of Women*; and Homans, *Bearing the Word*.

8. Levine, *Feminist Lives in Victorian England*, 46.

9. Bick contends that in the *Life* Gaskell is "attempting to effect the definitive separation between Charlotte the virtuous young woman and Charlotte's fictional heroines," who are characterized by rebelliousness, passion, and rage" ("Clouding the 'Severe Truth,'" 34).

10. Gaskell, *The Life of Charlotte Brontë*, 124; hereafter, page numbers are cited in parentheses in the text.

11. Holcombe, *Victorian Ladies at Work*, 14.

12. Lansbury, *Elizabeth Gaskell: The Novel of Social Crisis*, 17.

13. Gérin, *Elizabeth Gaskell*, 259.

14. Lansbury, *Elizabeth Gaskell: The Novel of Social Crisis*, 17, 18.

15. Weiss, "Elizabeth Gaskell," 276.

16. See "Women Writers and the Double Standard," in *Woman in Sexist Society*, ed. Vivian Gornick and Barbara Moran, 329.

17. Nestor, *Female Friendships and Communities*, 28.

18. Spacks says that Elizabeth Gaskell, like Jane Austen and George Eliot, raises questions about women's lot that she does not finally answer and concludes that she does not "because, clearly [she] cannot" (*The Female Imagination*, 317). In several of her letters, Gaskell makes it clear that she looks to the future for the resolution of some of the problems facing women of her age.

19. Nestor has recognized Gaskell's willingness to use her position to help other women writers and her tendency to identify herself as one of a community of women writers. But she avoids a discussion of the *Life*. See *Female Friendships and Communities*. For a classic statement about the female community, see Smith-Rosenberg's "The Female World of Love and Ritual."

Chapter 7

"Growing Fast into a Woman": *Wives and Daughters*

Throughout her career, Gaskell remained preoccupied with the issue of women's work.[1] In her earliest novel, *Mary Barton*, Gaskell focuses on a working-class character who engages in paid employment outside the home. *North and South* centers upon a middle-class woman, the daughter of a minister, who works, without pay, for social reform. *Cranford* deals with impoverished women who nevertheless manage to survive within their own village economy. In *The Life of Charlotte Brontë*, Gaskell treats the life of a middle-class woman who works as a governess and as a writer, all the while fulfilling her domestic duties as a daughter. In her last novel, *Wives and Daughters* (1866), Gaskell takes on the subtler task of sketching the life of a young woman whose financial security prevents her from accepting paid employment and whose gifts and circumstances do not lead her to an established, socially acceptable vocational path. The novel asks, What is a young woman like Molly Gibson to do?

In this novel, Gaskell returns to English village life as she examines the formation of identity for a middle-class girl. What kinds of models are available to her, what her models teach her, and what she is expected to do are all issues raised by the novel. Far from an evasive retreat into the private realm, *Wives and Daughters* is trenchant in its criticism of social attitudes toward women as it deplores the lack of real opportunities for women to pursue a meaningful vocation. *The Life of Charlotte Brontë* was written to champion a close friend; *Wives and Daughters*, as the title suggests, seems to have been written to champion her daughters, and all daughters, as they work to make a place for themselves in the public sphere.

Although *Wives and Daughters* has been regarded by some as the author's greatest achievement, critics have not always been enthusiastic about the novel's subject matter or its characters.[2] Although some have seen Molly as an essentially static, uninteresting character, I will argue that Molly does indeed develop in the course of the novel—from a naive girl to an experienced, discerning woman. Against a group of women that includes Miss Eyre, Mrs. Hamley, Lady Harriet, Hyacinth Gibson, Cynthia Kirkpatrick, the Misses Browning, Mrs.Goodenough, and Aimée Hamley, Molly must define herself. As she undergoes this process, she must learn to separate truth from falsehood, to recognize her own feelings, and, above all, to act as she sees fit, prepared for the consequences. Through her presentation of Molly, Gaskell is exploring the complexities of acquiring a female identity within Victorian culture.

From childhood, the Victorian middle-class girl was encouraged to prepare herself for her future role as wife and mother. During adolescence, she was encouraged to remain passive, as young men made their offers and pledged their undying devotion. While, occupied as he was with the practical realities of his vocation, courtship and marriage was only one part of a young man's life, for a young woman it was the central part. Most of her energies were turned inward as she engaged in a period of waiting for her destiny to work itself out. While young men were busy doing, young women were supposed to be content merely being. According to Deborah Gorham, becoming a woman meant "accepting limits and restraints, and recognizing male superiority."[3]

Gaskell had a different vision of what women could and should be. Unlike many other nineteenth-century novelists, Gaskell does not represent marriage as the only appropriate and satisfying choice for a woman. Perhaps because two of her daughters did not marry, Gaskell was sensitive to women's need for a purpose in life, a purpose that vocation could provide. Gaskell felt keenly for single women "who waken up some morning to the sudden feeling of the *purposelessness* of their life" (Letter 72). Gaskell's acknowledgment of the social realities that meant that a significant proportion of women would never marry led her to conclude that women must seek satisfying alternatives and to support women in their efforts to this end.

The opening of the novel captures Molly's dilemma in a suggestive scene: Molly is lying in bed, early in the morning, longing to get up, but reluctant to do so for fear of the scoldings of the servant, Betty. When she hears the church bells chime six o'clock, she jumps up and runs to the window, opening the casement to let in some air. With great economy, Gaskell hints at the energies Molly possesses; at the same time, she demonstrates how those energies are arbitrarily kept in check. The detail of the window is also significant, for windows in women's fiction often suggest boundaries and imprisonment. Molly's delight in the sound of the bell, which called "every one to their daily work," likewise points to her wish to participate in the world of work.[4] This is Molly as a young girl: restless, obedient, and alive to the possibilities of life.

Because Molly is motherless, her identity is first shaped by her interaction with her father. Mr. Gibson loves his daughter, but does not express his affection overtly; "his most caressing appellation for her was 'Goosey,' and he took a pleasure in bewildering her infant mind with his badinage" (63). Yet early on, Molly grows to understand her father, and although he teases her and quizzes her, she feels free to confide in him. The kind of relationship Molly has with her father challenges her intellectually and supports her emotionally; it is "half banter, half seriousness, but altogether confidential friendship" (64).

The early death of the mother and the identification with the father have been shown to be typical patterns in the lives of nonconforming women.[5] These patterns were true of Elizabeth Gaskell, and they are true of many of her characters. Because Molly is motherless, she learns to think and judge independently; without a mother to serve as her advocate and guide, Molly must stand up for herself. Furthermore, in her strong sympathy and admiration for her father, Molly strongly identifies with masculine ideals of action and achievement.

Yet Molly's father does not always recognize what his daughter needs or what she is capable of. Very early in the novel, the reader learns that Doctor Gibson underestimates his daughter's intellectual requirements. To Miss Eyre, Molly's governess, he gives the following instructions:

> Don't teach Molly too much; she must sew, and read, and write, and do her sums; but I want to keep her a child, and if I find more learning desirable for her, I'll see about giving it to her myself. After all, I'm not sure that reading or writing is necessary. Many a good woman gets married with only a cross instead of her name; it's rather a diluting of mother-wit, to my fancy; but, however, we must yield to the prejudices of society, Miss Eyre, and so you may teach the child to read. (65)

Here Mr. Gibson expresses the common Victorian attitude that too much learning is dangerous for women; his use of the term "mother-wit" is telling, for it suggests that women naturally have the "wit" to be mothers and that extensive education will deter women from their natural role, that is, that it will keep them from being good mothers. Following Mr. Gibson's instructions, Miss Eyre tries to keep Molly back in every branch of education, with the exception of reading and writing. Dr. Gibson's approach to his daughter's education contrasts sharply with Gaskell's own: the search for appropriate schools for her daughters is an important issue in her letters. The second daughter, Meta, probably the most intellectual, was sent to Harriet Martineau's school, where she received an education that exceeded the limits normally set for middle-class women. Not content with the usual curriculum for women, Martineau argued in *Household Education* that "the brain which will learn French will learn Greek," a language that was widely viewed as far too difficult for the feminine mind to grasp.[6] Even the daughters who were not intellectually inclined were not permitted to avoid difficult subjects. Gaskell warns her oldest daughter that if she becomes their tutor "they must do *hard & correct* as well as interesting work" (Letter 143). In the novel, on the other hand, the bright, interested student is held back because she happens to be a girl: the narrator says, "it was only by fighting and struggling hard, that bit by bit Molly persuaded her father to let her have French and drawing lessons" (65). Doctor Gibson's resistance to his daughter's education only increases her appetite for mental stimulation: "being daunted by her father in every intellectual attempt, she read every book that came in her way, almost with as much delight as if it had been forbidden" (65). Living in a society that sees learning as extraneous for women, Molly must fight for her education.

Not only does Molly's father attempt to limit her education; he also shelters her, hindering her social development. Because Molly grows up in a quiet, uneventful village, she lacks the experiences that would equip her for the complexities of adult life. As a result, when she is privileged enough to receive an invitation to the Towers, she is so overwhelmed that she retreats into the garden, only to fall asleep. Her extreme embarrassment at being caught napping and her extreme fear that she will be left at the Towers are both signs of her inexperience. When her father comes to take her home, she becomes almost hysterical; his surprised response to her behavior is, "Why, what a noodle you are, Molly!" (57). Ironically, Molly is chided for the state of arrested development that her father has fostered.

Again Gaskell's treatment of her daughters is quite different. From the beginning, she gave her young children the freedom to make some of their own choices. For instance, she speaks admiringly of her oldest, Marianne, as being a "law unto herself" (Letter 101). On a similar note, Gaskell mentions in a letter that after the nurse had come, five-year-old Florence "chose to go to the nursery to be dressed and has been playing about ever since" (Letter 21). As her daughters grew older, Gaskell allowed them to have active social lives. Marianne and Florence were in particular demand. In a letter to a friend, Gaskell remarks on the "1001 invitations . . . thronging in" (Letter 60). Gaskell furthermore encouraged her daughters to explore what the world had to offer through frequent travel; on one occasion, Gaskell accompanied her large household, servants included, to Europe—without her husband, who liked to take his holidays alone. Realizing that sheltering her children would be futile as well as unhealthy, Gaskell made every effort to equip them to act in the world—and to allow them to enter it.

In her portrayal of Molly's sheltered girlhood, Gaskell is criticizing the assumption of domestic ideology that women are fragile creatures who need constant supervision and protection. As Molly moves into young womanhood, her father continues to shield her from experience, particularly from romantic attention. One of his apprentices becomes enamoured of Molly and attempts to send her a love letter. When his messenger arouses his suspicions, Doctor Gibson intercepts the letter and handles the incident himself, sending the smitten young man a sarcastic prescription to cure his lovesickness. A meeting follows, in which Doctor Gibson initially announces his intention to remove Mr. Coxe from his household. Even Gibson realizes that he is overreacting, and modifies his stance by conceding that the young man can stay on the condition that he refrain from disclosing his feelings, by looks, acts, or words. This episode is profoundly shocking to the doctor, who is "startled at discovering that his little one was growing fast into a woman" and that he "could not guard her as he would have wished" (87). Years later, when Mr. Coxe returns to woo the now-eligible Molly, she is still completely ignorant of his feelings. Keeping his daughter unaware of situations that involve her, Doctor Gibson fails to assist Molly in her path toward womanhood. While Molly's father is helpful in some ways, he is harmful in others; Molly needs to observe female models and female patterns of conduct as she develops a social identity.

Gradually, Molly finds her place within a community of women. As she matures, she must assess the feminine models before her and choose for herself the values that will govern her own life.[7] Surrounded by various types of femininity, Molly learns to discern the bad from the good models, learning from both.

The governess, Miss Eyre, is an important early female presence in Molly's life. Perceived as a threat to her authority by the other servant in the household, Miss Eyre has to endure Betty's constant criticisms. Molly is quick to defend her governess, who greets these attacks with patience and refrains from retaliating. Sensing the injustice of the situation, Molly sides with Miss Eyre: when she is offered temptations to neglect Miss Eyre's wishes, "Molly steadily resisted, and plodded away at her task of sewing or her difficult sum" (66). When Betty makes jokes at her teacher's expense, Molly "looked up with the utmost gravity, as if requesting the explanation of an unintelligible speech" (66). And when Betty speaks impertinently to Miss Eyre herself, Molly "flew out in such a violent passion of words in defence of her silent trembling governess, that even Betty herself was daunted" (67).

Partly because of her youthful experiences, Molly is quick to perceive oppression and unfairness, and although she respects her governess, she does not approve of her submissive acceptance of injuries. Indeed, when Miss Eyre corrects Molly for giving way to temper, the child "thought it hard to be blamed for what she considered her just anger against Betty" (67). As she matures, Molly continues to stand up for women whom she believes to be wronged. Observing her governess shows Molly one kind of feminine response to oppression, a response that she rejects.

Molly also frequently visits with the Misses Browning, two neighbors "past their first youth," who take an interest in Molly because they had been fond of her mother (42). Well-meaning but simple-minded, the Brownings also fail as exemplars for Molly. Indeed, on important occasions they misjudge Molly and draw unfair conclusions about her behavior. As she matures, Molly must examine the values and standards that the Misses Browning exemplify and, rejecting what offends her, form her own.

From the time the Brownings are first introduced, Gaskell makes it clear that they are not women whom Molly should emulate. First of all, despite their advanced age, the Brownings are excessively preoccupied with dress. But it is apparent even to the unobservant Doctor Gibson that their dress is tasteless. When they kindly offer to lend Molly some accessories in preparation for her visit to the Towers, Doctor Gibson is "unwilling to have his child decked up according to their fancy; he esteemed his old servant Betty's as the more correct, because the more simple" (43). Long after the reason to do so has passed, the Misses Browning continue to dress to attract attention. When they are invited to the Towers, as if they are young girls, both have new dresses made. In contrast, not overly concerned about her looks, Molly wears a plain white dress; later in the novel she complains of "the dress, and the dressing, and the weariness the next day" that accompany a ball (355). Molly does not share her neighbors' inordinate attention to personal appearance.

Molly's sense of refinement also makes her notice the lack of refinement in the Brownings, the "coarser and louder tones in which they spoke, the provincialism of their pronunciation, the absence of interest in things, and their greediness of details about persons" (183). When Molly visits the Brownings after returning from Hamley Hall, she is uncomfortable with their probing questions about her new stepmother, as well as their insinuations about Roger Hamley. "You seem to have seen a great deal of Mr. Roger, Molly? said Miss Browning in a way intended to convey a great deal of meaning to her sister and none at all to Molly" (183). At first perplexed, and then embarrassed, Molly confronts Miss Browning, saying, "I can't help seeing what you fancy . . . but it is very wrong" (184). Molly is self-assertive enough to correct her elders when she sees that her relationship with Roger is being misconstrued: although Molly and Roger do later develop romantic feelings for each other, at this point the two only share a deep friendship, based on common interests. This conversation with Miss Browning compels Molly to define for herself and to articulate for others the nature of her relationship with Roger Hamley. In so doing, Molly separates herself from the narrow vision of the Brownings, who assume that any interaction between a man and a woman implies a romantic involvement. Male-female friendship allowed for the possibility of a relationship between men and women that was not based on courtship, courtship being the principal vocation of girls of Molly's age and class. It is important to note here that Gaskell herself had many male friends and carried on a long correspondence with an American whom she met on a trip to Rome, Charles Norton. Gaskell was obviously comfortable in the presence of men, as she writes in a letter to Catherine Winkworth, "I wish I could help taking to men so much more than to women . . . and I wish I could help men taking to me" (Letter 633). The repetition of the phrase "I wish" suggests that Gaskell, like Molly, was acquainted with the negative public perceptions of even nonromantic relationships.

Gaskell focuses on such a misunderstanding when Molly is seen with Mr. Preston and rumors begin to fly.[8] The talk becomes so loud that the Brownings learn of the scandal, and, instead of approaching Molly for an explanation, the elder Miss Browning takes it upon herself to inform Doctor Gibson of the gossip regarding his daughter. Convinced that Molly is indeed guilty, Miss Browning, along with all of Hollingford, slights the innocent girl, speaking to her "with chilling dignity, and much reserve" (573). Everyone, including Miss Browning, "was civil to her, but no one was cordial; there was a very perceptible film of difference in their behavior to her from what it was formerly" (573). The Misses Browning wrongly judge by appearances and fail to offer support in a crisis.

Rejection by her neighbors is trying to Molly, but at the same time it allows her to demonstrate her strength of character and her maturity. As young as she is, Molly counsels her own father, who is also affected by the scandal: "Dear, dear papa, I'm sure it is best to take no notice of these speeches . . . . By-and-by they'll forget how much they made out of so little" (570). In the meantime Molly exercises patience, comforted by the knowledge that "it would be much worse if [she] really had been doing wrong" (572). Molly's ostracism teaches her the possible consequences of acting in a society that does not recommend action for women. Mrs. Goodenough expresses the conventional Victorian attitude: "Women should mind what they're about, and never be talked of" (559). In her portrait of Molly, Gaskell is challenging the values of a society that views action as compromising. Through Molly, Gaskell suggests that public appearances are not always accurate.

Through the character of Hyacinth Gibson, Gaskell evokes the other side of the paradox: that social correctness does not always indicate moral integrity. Molly's stepmother is perhaps her most omnipresent model of femininity. On the surface, Hyacinth appears to be the ideal Victorian woman. Highly respected by Lord and Lady Cumnor, she was "ready to talk, when a little trickle of conversation was required; so willing to listen, and to listen with tolerable intelligence" (130). "About novels and poetry, travels and gossip, personal details, or anecdotes of any kind, she always made exactly the remarks which are expected from an agreeable listener" (130). With her soft, large blue eyes and auburn hair, her becoming dress, her pleasant voice, and her polished manners, Hyacinth presents a conventional image of womanhood. Yet Gaskell quickly demonstrates how far Hyacinth falls short as a model for Molly by revealing how Hyacinth's public self-presentation is at odds with her private self.[9]

Unlike Molly, who remarks that she would rather be a housekeeper than a lady, Hyacinth regards work as degrading and associates marriage with leisure. At the same time, she is careful to cultivate the image of herself as willing to labor endlessly for others. Daydreaming over a book, Hyacinth thinks "how pleasant it would be to have a husband once more;—some one who would work while she sat at her elegant ease in a prettily-furnished drawing room" (138). Instead of deriving a sense of fulfillment from her labor, Hyacinth resents having to work and even regards work as unnatural for women: "I wonder if I am to go on all my life toiling and moiling for money? It's not natural. Marriage is the natural thing; then the husband has all that kind of dirty work to do, and his wife sits in the drawing-room like a lady" (131). Unlike Gaskell, who was concerned lest one of her daughters "fall into 'young-lady-life,'" Hyacinth cherishes the idea of leisure (Letter 476). Relief that she will no longer have to struggle to earn her own livelihood is Hyacinth's response when Doctor Gibson proposes marriage. Above all, Hyacinth values her comfort.

In her depiction of Hyacinth, Gaskell points to the hypocrisy that often results from the Victorian ideal of sacrificial service. While she covertly seeks to attain a comfortable life for herself, Hyacinth only pretends to attend to others. Once engaged, she makes plans for a speedy wedding, notwithstanding her responsibilities to her pupils. Secretly hoping that Doctor Gibson will urge her to give up her position, she prepares a little speech for him, strong enough to overcome the scruples that she felt she ought to have at telling the parents of her pupils that she does not intend to return to school. When her fiancé does not cooperate with her plans, but actually suggests that it would not be right to leave in the middle of the term, Hyacinth claims that she cannot bear to think of his having no one to look after him. In this scene Hyacinth pretends to be the perfect Victorian wife, who, according to Sarah Ellis, should spend her time "devising means for promoting the happiness of others, while her own derives a remote and secondary existence from theirs."[10] In fact, Hyacinth's speech is hollow—as hollow as the ideal itself.[11] Pretense is typical of Hyacinth, who constantly masks her selfish motives as altruism.

Moreover, Gaskell uses Hyacinth to attack the ruthless pursuit of marriage that women are reduced to in a culture that equates marriage with their success. Manipulation is second nature to Hyacinth Gibson. Aware that a marriage with Osborne Hamley would be socially advantageous, Mrs. Gibson tries to create opportunities in which her daughter Cynthia can display her charms. On the day the young people first meet, the ambitious mother gives away her scheme by the contented look that appears on her face as Osborne begins to address his remarks to her daughter: "All at once [Molly] perceived that Mrs. Gibson would not dislike a marriage between Osborne and Cynthia" (268). However, when Hyacinth overhears her husband discussing Osborne's precarious health with another doctor, she quickly recalculates, concluding that in the event of Osborne's death, his younger brother, Roger, may do as well. Therefore, Mrs. Gibson turns her attention to Roger, whom she had previously called "as heavy as heavy can be. A great awkward fellow . . . who looks as if he did not know two and two made four" (274). Her constant plots to throw Cynthia and Roger together are so transparent that "Molly chafed at the net spread so evidently, and at Roger's blindness in coming so willingly to be entrapped" (390). Molly finds her stepmother's machinations repugnant. Nor does she admire Cynthia's passive cooperation with her mother's plans. Imagining herself in such a situation, Molly "felt as if she could not have acted as Cynthia did" (390). Molly says to herself that she "would have resisted; have gone out, for instance, when she was expected to stay at home; or have lingered in the garden when a long country walk was planned" (390-1). In response to a neighbor's suggestion that Mrs. Gibson should turn her attention to Molly next, Molly responds, "half angry, half laughing; 'when I want to be married, I'll not trouble mamma. I'll look out for myself'" (681).

Although Molly's new stepmother presents herself as a person of deep feeling, she is in fact cold and unfeeling. When Mrs. Hamley becomes ill and wishes to see Molly, the squire comes to the Gibson household to bring Molly back with him. Despite the urgency of the request, Mrs. Gibson refuses to allow Molly to go, reminding her that they are to go visiting together that night. In this incident, Mrs. Gibson places a social call before the needs of a sick neighbor, saying that "an engagement is an engagement" (224). And on a similar occasion, when Cynthia notes how ill Osborne Hamley has been looking, Mrs. Gibson shakes her head ominously and predicts that the young man will not live long, going on in the next breath to speculate on the effect Osborne's death will have on Roger and Cynthia's marriage date. Cynthia, shocked, murmurs, "Don't speak of that in the same breath as Osborne's life, mamma" (475). In defense, Mrs. Gibson points out, "One can't help following out one's thoughts. People must die, you know—young, as well as old" (475).

Gradually, Molly senses the fundamental dishonesty of her stepmother's conduct and wonders what to do about it.

> At first she made herself uncomfortable with questioning herself as to how far it was right to leave unnoticed the small domestic failings—the webs, the distortions of truth which had prevailed in their household ever since her father's second marriage. She knew that very often she longed to protest, but did not do it, from the desire of sparing her father any discord; and she saw by his face that he, too, was occasionally aware of certain things that gave him pain, as showing that his wife's standard of conduct was not as high as he would have liked. It was a wonder to Molly whether this silence was right or wrong. (407)

Sometimes Molly's directness effectively counters her stepmother's duplicity. On one occasion, when Mrs. Gibson is recovering from a cold, Molly is asked to pass up an invitation to a party and stay with her stepmother. At the last minute, Mrs. Gibson declares that she is feeling better and would like to see Molly dressed for the party. Molly insists that she would rather not go, and her stepmother says in reproach, "Very well! Only I think it is rather selfish of you, when you see I am so willing to make the sacrifice for your sake" (574). Molly innocently points out the inconsistency of her stepmother's words: "But you say it is a sacrifice to you, and I don't want to go," at which point she is told not to "chop logic" (574). In most instances refraining from directly contradicting her stepmother, Molly challenges her standards merely by always speaking the truth. Coral Lansbury points out that "it is Molly who sees clearly and speaks plainly, her goodness is not passive, a denial of action, but the positive force in the novel."[12]

While Molly genuinely loves her stepsister, Cynthia, she soon becomes aware that, like her mother, Cynthia "was not remarkable for unflinching morality" (255). Therefore, while Molly develops a close relationship with her stepsister, Cynthia, too, fails as an appropriate model for Molly to emulate. Aware that she possesses an "unconscious power of fascination," Cynthia, above all, wishes to please (254). This fascination stems in part from Cynthia's protean nature, her ability to adapt her personality to various people.[13] Nevertheless, she lacks the capacity to love deeply, telling Molly, "I've not the gift of loving; . . . I can respect, and I fancy I can admire, and I can like, but I never feel carried off my feet by love for any one" (422). Despite her emotional disengagement, Cynthia deliberately and knowingly accedes to the marriage game, eliciting three serious proposals from men whom she does not love.[14] In contrast, Molly feels deeply and is loyal to those with whom she forms close bonds. Molly's genuine grief over Mrs. Hamley's death makes Cynthia conscious of her own deficiency and prompts her to remark to Molly, "I wish I could love people as you do, Molly!" (257).

Cynthia's treatment of the man Molly grows to love, Roger Hamley, reveals the differences between the two young women. When she first meets Roger, Cynthia turns eyes "of childlike innocence and wonder about them, which did not quite belong to Cynthia's character" (277). Putting on her "armour of magic that evening," Cynthia casts a spell over Roger, who "fell most prone and abject" (277). This Cynthia does, not because she cares for Roger, but because "she could not help trying her power on strangers" (277). In contrast, Molly is truly interested in Roger's plans and projects and longs to hear the details of his academic progress, which he shares with Cynthia. While Cynthia protects herself from emotional experience by toying with men, Molly risks the pain that can accompany caring.

Despite the negative models of womanhood all around her, Molly also meets women who provide the kind of guidance that she needs to develop into a clear-sighted, strong, capable woman. Mrs. Hamley, Aimée Hamley, and Lady Harriet Cumnor are all positive influences who show Molly what she can do and be. Nancy Chodorow has argued that girls who are surrounded by a strong network of female relatives and female friends tend to develop a strong sense of selfhood. With the support of caring women, Molly achieves self-knowledge and self-confidence.

Before she becomes acquainted with Molly, Mrs. Hamley's life is unfulfilled. A "delicate fine London lady," Mrs. Hamley married Roger Hamley, a country squire (73). Accustomed to a cultivated life in the city, Mrs. Hamley gradually gives up her trips to London when her husband fails to show an interest in what she had seen and done on each trip: "she gave up her sociable pleasure in the company of her fellows in education and position," and, "deprived of all her strong interests, she sank into ill-health; nothing definite; only she never was well" (74). Gaskell makes clear Squire Hamley's role in the poor health of his wife: "they were very happy, though possibly Mrs. Hamley would not have sunk into the condition of a chronic invalid, if her husband had cared a little more for her various tastes, or allowed her the companionship of those who did" (73). Cut off from the people and the pursuits that had engaged her, Mrs. Hamley spends most of her life on a sofa, "alternately reading and composing verse" (76).

Molly's visits to Hamley Hall at Mrs. Hamley's invitation lead to a mutually satisfying friendship between the motherless girl and the sickly woman who had lost a daughter long before. Mrs. Hamley provides a kind of nurturing that Molly has lacked. After she welcomes Molly into her home, Mrs. Hamley predicts, " I think we shall be great friends" (94). Putting Molly in a room close to her own, confiding in Molly about her well-loved sons, and sharing with Molly her pleasure in poetry, Mrs. Hamley treats her like a daughter.

Equally important, Mrs. Hamley gives Molly something to do. During her visit, Molly performs all of the duties that would have fallen to a daughter of the house, making breakfast, reading the newspaper aloud to the squire, strolling over the gardens with him, gathering fresh flowers to fill the drawing-room, and serving as a companion to Mrs. Hamley on her drives. In return, Mrs. Hamley is sensitive to Molly's feelings, steering conversations away from painful topics like the death of Molly's mother and the possible remarriage of her father; moreover, she is responsive to Molly's interests, leaving her free to browse in the well-stocked library.

In her portrait of Mrs. Hamley, Gaskell is by no means recommending a life of invalidism. At the same time, she is sympathetic to her character, who, separated by marriage from the round of activities in the city, languishes into debility in an isolated setting. Through Mrs. Hamley, Gaskell is calling attention to the limited range of options available to the middle-class woman.

Gaskell also makes it clear that Mrs. Hamley is not idle: what she can do, she does. What she does primarily is to mother Molly. In the scenes between Molly and Mrs. Hamley, Gaskell affirms the value of maternal care. As she serves Mrs. Hamley, Molly both receives and gives nurturance, an activity that contemporary feminists like Carol Gilligan have seen as quintessentially feminine.[15] Moreover, Mrs. Hamley teaches Molly the powerful influence a woman can exercise over her family. Gaskell makes the point explicit: "Quiet and passive as Mrs. Hamley had always been in appearance, she was the ruling spirit of the house" (285). After Mrs. Hamley's death, Roger invites Molly to the Hall, sensing that Molly, like his mother, could "put us a little to rights" (284). Thus her visits to Hamley Hall form an essential part of Molly's education as a woman.

Lady Harriet represents a very different model of womanhood. Wendy Craik

says approvingly that Lady Harriet is "remarkable and wholly convincing as an
independent-minded, mature woman with no impulse toward marriage, witty,
intelligent, and outspoken."[16]   Lady Harriet responds favorably to Molly
because she senses her own qualities in the straightforward girl. When Molly
goes to visit at the Towers after the marriage of her father, Lady Harriet
immediately initiates a conversation on the subject she knows is foremost on
Molly's mind: her father's remarriage. Trying to console Molly, Lady Harriet
says of Molly's new stepmother, her own former governess, "She always let me
have my own way, and I've no doubt she'll let you have yours" (193). She
goes on to warn Molly about her stepmother's manipulative nature, recalling
how as a girl she used to think that she was managing her governess, until one
day she realized that her governess was managing her.   Molly responds
indignantly, "I should hate to be managed" (195). Despite their differences in
class, Molly and Lady Harriet share a love of independence; this affinity sparks
a friendship that becomes important to both of them.

Lady Harriet's self-assured fearlessness is instructive to Molly, who gathers
the courage to assert herself before her new friend.   When Lady Harriet
proposes a visit to the Brownings, Molly quietly says that it would be best if she
did not call on her neighbors. Because Lady Harriet respects Molly, she allows
herself to be reproved by the girl, who disapproves of the half-joking,
condescending way in which Lady Harriet refers to her friends as "Pecksy and
Flapsy."   "Speaking quite gravely," Lady Harriet apologizes for her
thoughtlessness, thereby sealing the newly-formed bond between the two women
(199). Lady Harriet makes a favorite of Molly, seeking her out in her own
home and in social settings.[17]

Furthermore, Lady Harriet teaches Molly the important skill of managing
men.   When Mr. Preston, her father's land agent, makes the mistake of
presuming intimacy with Lady Harriet, inviting her to look at some alterations
he had made in the garden, he is coolly dismissed.   Stinging from Lady
Harriet's rejection, he repeats his invitation to Molly, only to be expressly sent
away for the evening. Lady Harriet reinforces her actions with a word of
caution: "I've an instinctive aversion to him; . . . and I desire you don't allow
him ever to get intimate with you" (198). Lady Harriet's lesson comes back to
Molly later in the novel when Molly agrees to be an advocate for her stepsister,
Cynthia, who at sixteen had become financially indebted to Preston. Following
Lady Harriet's example, Molly takes charge of the situation, interrupting Preston
when he is impertinent and threatening to expose him by telling all to Lady
Harriet and by asking her to speak to her father, Lord Cumnor.   Molly's
strategy is effective: Preston, forced to admit that the letters he was holding over
Cynthia would compromise himself as well as her, has no other choice but to
return them. As she watches Lady Harriet, Molly learns how to remain in
control while dealing with men.

It is Lady Harriet who rescues Molly from public scandal by taking her under her personal protection. Unlike the Brownings, Lady Harriet expresses faith in Molly, despite appearances. Aware of the advantages of her class, Lady Harriet first demands to know Preston's intentions toward Molly and then accompanies Molly on a conspicuous walk through the length of the town, loitering at Grinstead's for half an hour and leaving cards at the Brownings'. Lady Harriet's public support of Molly is of course intended to restore Molly in Hollingford's favor. This scene is an interesting variation on the stock image of a woman being vindicated by a man; in Gaskell's version, a woman is vindicated by another woman. Lady Harriet's actions demonstrate to Molly that women can be their own champions, that they need not rely on Prince Charming or a knight on horseback.

Aimée Hamley is likewise a positive figure for Molly. Patsy Stoneman calls Aimée a "genuine working woman with practical skills."[18] Aimée is self-sufficient, supporting herself by working as a nursemaid. Entering into a secret marriage with Osborne Hamley, Aimée continues to live independently, only enjoying intermittent visits from her husband. When news of Osborne's ill health reaches Aimée, she packs up and, despite his instructions, journeys to Hollingsford, along with their young child.[19] Although she is scarcely older than Molly, Aimée relies on her own judgment and makes up her mind on what course of action to follow.

Molly is eventually able to put into practice the lessons in nurturing and self-reliance she learns from her more constructive role models. Strong and competent though Aimée is, when she learns of her husband's death, she is overtaken by grief, and it becomes Molly's job to care for the young mother. In this time of crisis, Molly offers a sympathetic presence, placing Aimée in a quiet room and checking on her from time to time. Indeed, Molly's father entrusts her with the whole household, at the same time recognizing that she is "young for the work" (607). Declaring that she will stay the night, Molly is confident enough of her own powers to say, "I can manage" (608). In the aftermath of Osborne's death, Molly reenacts the kind of caring that she received from Mrs. Hamley. Furthermore, following the example of Lady Harriet, she defends the Frenchwoman, whose nationality, status as a servant, and religious affiliation all make her vulnerable to criticism.

Molly's response to trials wins her masculine approval and respect. Squire Hamley, the first to see Molly's value, writes in a note to her father, "Molly is a treasure" (232). Osborne comes to realize that the secret of his marriage is safe with Molly. When Osborne dies, Doctor Gibson turns to Molly to notify the young wife. After the ordeal of Mrs. Hamley's death, soon followed by Osborne's, Molly finally collapses, from "exhausting work."[20] During her period of illness, her father realizes, more fully than he ever has before, her worth: "He felt as if he should not know what to do without Molly" (636). And, by the end of the novel, Roger Hamley understands that it is Molly, not Cynthia, who deserves his love.[21]

The relationship between Molly and Roger is based on similar inclinations and interests. When Molly visits the Towers as a child, she is suffocated by its air of formality and begs to go into the garden, where she can breathe freely. Throughout the novel, Molly takes long walks, observing nature closely and finding pleasure there. In like manner, Roger is such a lover of nature that he instinctively avoids treading unnecessarily on plants. While Molly is visiting at Hamley Hall, Roger stimulates Molly's interest in nature by setting out his microscope and some objects he has collected as well as by offering her scientific books. Later, Mrs. Gibson comments on Molly's reading "such deep books—all about facts and figures" (307). Mrs. Gibson is no great intellect, but even scholars are impressed with Molly. When Molly is introduced to the learned Lord Hollingford at a ball, she makes a favorable impression on the scholarly man, who exclaims, "What a charming little lady! . . . Most girls of her age are so difficult to talk to; but she is intelligent and full of interest in all sorts of sensible things; well read, too—she was up in *Le Regne Animal*" (339).[22] It is true that Roger first acts as a mentor to Molly, but it is equally true that she quickly becomes capable of mentally challenging her tutor: "Sometimes her remarks had probed into his mind, and excited him to the deep thought in which he delighted" (182).

In fact, Molly at times takes the role of teacher, showing Roger the limits of conventional wisdom about self-sacrifice and self-control. When Roger tries to console Molly about her father's remarriage, offering her platitudes about thinking of others before herself, Molly retorts, "It will be very dull when I shall have killed myself, as it were, and live only in trying to do, and to be, as other people like. I don't see any end to it. I might as well never have lived" (170). And when he suggests that in ten years this trial will seem unimportant, Molly reminds Roger of the urgency of the present and the primacy of individual human experience: "I daresay it seems foolish; perhaps all our earthly trials will appear foolish to us after a while; perhaps they seem so now to angels. But we are ourselves, you know, and this is now, not some time to come, a long, long way off. And we are not angels, to be comforted by seeing the ends for which everything is sent" (170).

The scenes between Roger and Molly point to the restrictions faced by a middle-class girl. Gaskell heightens the pair's contrasting prospects by emphasizing what they have in common. By juxtaposing Roger with Molly, Gaskell makes it clear that, although she has the potential, Molly has no real opportunity to pursue her intellectual interests. In contrast, Roger's intellectual gifts win him the title of senior wrangler at Cambridge, an honor that starts him on the path toward a distinguished career as a naturalist.[23] *Wives and Daughters* addresses the complex issue of gender identity by drawing the lives of two young people who are very much alike but who can expect two very different careers. Even before Roger settles on a vocation, he is confident that he will be able to give free rein to his talents: "He looked forward to an active life . . . He knew what were his talents and his tastes; and did not wish the former to lie buried, nor the latter, which he regarded as gifts, fitting him for some peculiar work, to be disregarded or thwarted" (391). Molly, on the other hand, experiences limitation and confinement. As a young girl, she makes the perceptive comparison of herself to a "lighted candle when they're putting the extinguisher on it" (58).[24]

Appropriately enough, Gaskell's last novel was never finished; nor are the problems it addresses ever completely resolved. With the help of positive models, Molly grows into a thoughtful, truthful woman—no slight accomplishment in a society that discouraged mental exertion and, by emphasizing appearances, encouraged dissimulation. At the end of the novel, Molly is clearly headed toward a marriage with Roger, with whom she is well matched. A sensitive, caring man, Roger will no doubt make Molly a satisfactory husband. Throughout the novel, Roger has acknowledged female competence, looking to Molly for help and guidance at critical moments in his life. Likewise, Roger exhibits trust in his sister-in-law: when his father asserts his claim over Osborne's child, Roger supports Aimée's superior skill in managing the child and helps make arrangements that will allow her to have authority over her child. There is every indication that Molly's choice of a husband is sound.

The last glimpse of Molly and Roger hints at the promise of their marriage: Roger, having been exposed to scarlet fever, cannot say goodbye to the Gibsons, so he is forced to wait underneath a tree, in the pouring rain, in hopes that one of the family will see him out the window. When Mrs. Gibson spots him, he begins to wave, and Molly "responded to his sign" (702). After Molly's stepmother finally moves away from the window, they share a final goodbye, as they wave their handkerchiefs, the only object visible at a great distance. This scene suggests the success of private arrangements, private communication, which can, over time, effect changes in the public domain.[25] As in *The Princess*, when the prince sketches out the social possibilities of equality between the sexes and urges Princess Ida, "Let us type them now / In our own lives" (7, ll. 282-3), so Gaskell suggests that social change begins with the individual family unit.

No doubt, Molly will become a wife; very likely she will have a daughter. Gaskell's last novel points to the redeeming possibility of a marriage to an enlightened man and, as the title suggests, the transmission of a liberating female identity from wives to their daughters.

Notes

1. Bonaparte asserts that "Gaskell did not develop in time" and that her mind "resembled a wheel turning around and around continually" (*The Gypsy-Bachelor of Manchester*, 14).

2. Wright devalues *Wives and Daughters* by saying that it deals "largely with emotional matters" and that its plot "develops round love stories and family crises" (*Mrs. Gaskell*, 226). Ganz calls the novel "unduly drawn out and basically static" (*Elizabeth Gaskell*, 164). Craik finds the main character, Molly Gibson, less than compelling; according to Craik, Molly is "endowed with no outstanding qualities of mind or heart" and "makes no spiritual and moral progress to wisdom" (*Elizabeth Gaskell and the English Provincial Novel*, 245). Spacks (*The Female Imagination*) and Stoneman (*Elizabeth Gaskell*), are much more positive about *Wives and Daughters*, as well as more perceptive about Gaskell's main interest in the novel. Stoneman has identified the structure of families and the socialization of girls—not romance—as the central subject matter of the novel. Furthermore, Stoneman argues that the novel "makes a thorough critique of female socialisation," which required Victorian women to be pretty and charming and which often made them calculating and manipulative (40). Spacks recognizes the essential problem faced by Molly Gibson: she has very little to do. Unlike the men in the novel, who "struggle to find time for all they wish to accomplish," Molly "struggles to fill her time" (89). Both critics see Gaskell as critical of a society that limits women's pursuits to courtship and marriage. While Reddy sees Molly as "likable but unremarkable," she views her ordinariness as "an important part of Gaskell's strategy" since it "prevents the reader from explaining away Molly's dissatisfaction and confusion as the predictable result of an extraordinary woman's equally predictable conflict with the conventional mores of her society" ("Men, Women, and Manners in *Wives and Daughters*," in *Reading and Writing Women's Lives: A Study of the Novel of Manners*, ed. Bege K. Bowers and Barbara Brothers, 69).

3. See Gorham for a general account of girlhood during the nineteenth century (*The Victorian Girl and the Feminine Ideal*, 101).

4. *Wives and Daughters*, 35; hereafter, page numbers are cited in parentheses in the text.

5. See Martin, "'No Angel in the House,'" and Showalter, *A Literature of Their Own*.

6. Martineau, *Household Education*, 271.

7. See Eifrig, "Growing Out of Motherhood." Eifrig asserts that Molly grows over the course of the novel, "developing both a discrimination about others and a confidence in her own character" (109).

8. Schor identifies silence as an important theme in the novel, which affects all the women characters in one way or another. As she puts it, "constant silence is seen as essential to women's lives" (199). According to Schor, "both Molly's 'good' concealment of suffering and Cynthia's more suspect deception about past failings suggest that in this world of limited female power, most women must lead painfully silent lives" (*Scheherezade in the Marketplace*, 200).

9. Recently, Langland has argued that it was the business of middle-class wives to manage and to advance the class position of their families. She offers a new reading of Hyacinth Gibson, which sees her as "an executive who knows her business" and who is successful at it ("Nobody's Angels," 301).

10. Ellis, *The Women of England*, 16.

11. Homans identifies Hyacinth Gibson with a language in which "words do not tell truths or accurately convey messages but, rather, enter into a free play of signifiers as figuration" (*Bearing the Word*, 258).

12. See *Elizabeth Gaskell: The Novel of Social Crisis*, 204.

13. Lansbury says that Cynthia "demands admiration without judgment because . . . [she] knows what she is and can find refuge from herself only in the reflected approval of others" (*Elizabeth Gaskell*, 120).

14. Schor comments that the lesson of the mother figures in the novel is that "to be female is primarily to be an invalid, to be passive, to suffer victimization" (*Scheherezade in the Marketplace*, 190). She goes on to say that "this is what both women try to overcome: Molly by defying Preston and, eventually, her father; Cynthia, by trying to write her own marriage plot, choosing and jilting men" (190).

15. See Gilligan, *In a Different Voice*.

16. *Elizabeth Gaskell and the English Provincial Novel*, 252-3.

17. Reddy identifies an interesting correspondence between Cynthia and Lady Harriet, who both "can see themselves simultaneously from the inside and the outside, each woman manipulating appearances at will but always recognizing her inner self as separable from others' views of her" ("Men, Women, and Manners in *Wives and Daughters*," 80).

18. Stoneman, *Elizabeth Gaskell*, 199.

19. Davis, "Feminist Critics and Literary Mothers," focuses on the burdensome aspect of motherhood when she notes the references to the weight of the child Aimée must carry alone. This reading brings to mind a similar pattern in *Jane Eyre*, when mental anguish is signified by Jane's dreams of carrying a crying child.

20. Stoneman, *Elizabeth Gaskell*, 188. Davis is troubled by Gaskell's use of breakdowns to give her heroines the "rest and solitude the characters of the novel will not give her" ("Feminist Critics and Literary Mothers," 525). I regard Gaskell's inclusion of such scenes as a criticism of a society which both overworks women and ignores their stress.

21. Unlike Craik, who views Molly as "unusually passive for a heroine" (*Elizabeth Gaskell and the English Provincial Novel*, 246), Lansbury perceives that it is Molly "who brings both her father and Roger Hamley to a better understanding of human nature through the recognition of herself as a unique and very remarkable young woman" (*Elizabeth Gaskell*, 197).

22. See Horn, *Education in Rural England, 1800-1914*, for a helpful overview of what kind of education middle-class girls like Molly would have received.

23. Critics have found a resemblance between Roger and the young Charles Darwin, who was in fact a relative of Gaskell's. Schor notes that "Gaskell had met Darwin several times, and his sister had traveled with Gaskell's daughter Meta to the Alps on a sketching tour" (*Scheherezade in the Marketplace*, 196).

24. Molly's plight is reminiscent of that faced by Dickens' Louisa Gradgrind, who is likewise frustrated by the possession of intellect in a society that does not approve of intellectual women. The image comparing the girl with a candle about to be snuffed out is, strangely enough, also the same.

25. Spacks credits Gaskell for a "rather searching investigation of the feminine situation," yet remarks that "it is not at all apparent what the answers are to the dilemmas she reveals" (*The Female Imagination*, 95). Spacks overlooks the hope implicit in the ending of the novel, calling the good marriage "only a hypothesis in this book; hardly that, even: a vague fantasy" and asking about Roger, "What is she to do with him, how is she to live?" (94). Reddy paints a similarly bleak picture of the ending when she claims that Gaskell is implying that there is no way for women to achieve actual happiness within social boundaries and that "this social problem seems insoluble" ("Men, Women, and Manners in *Wives and Daughters*," 85).

Chapter 8

Conclusion

Lord David Cecil's famous assessment of Elizabeth Gaskell as the quintessential Victorian woman overlooks much of what is interesting about the writer. Gaskell saw herself much more accurately, describing herself once as an "improper woman" (Letter 150). In a letter to Catherine Winkworth, Gaskell relates how she initiated a discussion of Sir Walter Scott's novels on a Sunday afternoon, thereby shocking one of her guests. Dismissing the negative reaction, Gaskell writes, "So there I am in a scrape—well! it can't be helped. I am myself and nobody else, and can't be bound by another's rules" (Letter 32). Gaskell's willingness to challenge the assumptions of her culture, particularly in regard to received ideas about the role of women in the workplace, makes her an engaging figure for twentieth-century readers.

Hilary Schor rejects the view of Gaskell as intellectually limited, conventional, and politically tame and argues instead that she was a woman of considerable intellectual sophistication who was conversant with the important issues of her day.[1] According to Schor, Gaskell's chief aim was to confront the literary plots she had inherited and to reimagine them, from a female point of view. Writing fiction for those denied a voice within the official culture, Schor is convinced, led Gaskell to an "awareness of her own silencing."

Once Gaskell discovered that her vocation was writing, she was faced with many forms of silencing, not the least of which was family responsibilities. A twentieth century spokesperson for the working class, Tillie Olsen, points out that of the women we remember from the previous century "nearly all never married (Jane Austen, Emily Brontë, Christina Rossetti, Emily Dickinson, Louisa May Alcott, Sarah Orne Jewett) or married late in their thirties (George Eliot, Elizabeth Barrett Browning, Charlotte Brontë, Olive Schreiner)."[2] Olsen can only think of four (George Sand, Harriet Beecher Stowe, Helen Hunt Jackson, and Elizabeth Gaskell) who married and had children as young women. Virginia Woolf wanted a room of her own; Elizabeth Gaskell wrote in a dining room with doors opening into all parts of the house, and commented longingly to her friend Charles Norton, "If I had a library like yours, all undisturbed for hours, how I would write!" (Letter 384). In a letter to her friend Ellen Nussey, Gaskell remarks, "I wrote twenty pages yesterday because it rained perpetually, and I was uninterrupted; such a good day for writing may not come again for months" (Letter 294). It is most frequently to close friends that Gaskell complains of the "sick wearied feeling of being over-worked" (Letter 308) and describes the multitude of tasks which she must handle simultaneously:

> But you see everybody comes to me perpetually. Now in this hour since breakfast I have had to decide on the following variety of important questions. Boiled beef—how long to boil? What perennials will do in Manchester smoke, & what colours our garden wants? Length of skirt for a gown? Salary of a nursery governess, & stipulations for a certain quantity of time to be left to herself.—Read letters on the state of Indian army—lent me by a very agreeable neighbour & return them, with a proper note, & as many wise remarks as would come in a hurry. Settle 20 questions of dress for the girls, who are going out for the day; & want to look nice & yet not spoil their gowns with the mud &c &c—See a lady about a MS story of hers, & give her disheartening but very good advice. Arrange about selling two poor cows for one good one,—see purchasers, & show myself up to cattle questions, keep, & prices—and it's not 1/2 past 10 yet! (Letter 384)

Gaskell's letter is dated 1857. Let us listen to a similar complaint from 1965:

> A full extended family life; the world of my job (transcriber in a dairy-equipment company); and the writing, which I was somehow able to carry around within me through work, through home. Time on the bus, even when I had to stand, was enough; the stolen moments at work, enough; the deep night hours for as long as I could stay awake, after the kids were in bed, after the household tasks were done, sometimes during. It is no accident that the first work I considered publishable began: "I stand here ironing, and what you asked me moved tormented back and forth with the iron."[3]

As Olsen has testified, "work interrupted, deferred, postponed makes blockage—at best, lesser accomplishment." Gaskell wrote only about half the number of books Dickens wrote. Anyone who reads her letters may wonder how she managed that. A still unresolved problem for women is a lack of time to do their work.

Another problem that is equally dispiriting is fear—the paralyzing fear of disapproval. Virginia Woolf praises women writers like Jane Austen and Emily Brontë who were able to overcome the fear and to speak their own truth: "What genius, what integrity it must have required in face of all that criticism, in the midst of that purely patriarchal society, to hold fast to the thing as they saw it without shrinking."[4] The difficulty Woolf refers to was all too familiar to

Gaskell, who nevertheless developed strategies for breaking out of silence. Frequently the aftermath of publication found Gaskell in a state of anxiety, even physical illness. Writing to Anne Robson after *Ruth* appeared, Gaskell confides, "how I shrink with more pain than I can tell you from what people are saying, though I wd do every jot of it over again to-morrow" (Letter 148). And to Eliza Fox, she relates, "I have been *so* ill; I do believe it has been a 'Ruth' fever" (Letter 150). Silence would have been so much easier for Gaskell: about *The Life of Charlotte Brontë* she said, "I was under a solemn promise to write the Life,—although I shrank from the task" (Letter 347a). Gaskell knew that to work is to risk; furthermore, she learned to authorize *herself* in her work: "I believe *now* I hit as near the truth as any one *could* do. And I weighed every line with all my whole power & heart, so that every line should go to its great purpose" (Letter 352).

With such daunting obstructions to their work, Gaskell recognized that for many women self-authorization is hard to achieve. One thing that seems to have sustained her is her relationships within the female community. In a response to an aspiring writer, Gaskell asks, "Have you no sister or relation who could come & help you for a little while till you get stronger,—no older friend at hand who would help you to plan your work so that it should oppress you as little as possible?" (Letter 515). To Anne Robson and Eliza Fox, Gaskell often confided her anxieties about both family and vocation, finding it a relief to articulate her worries and self-doubts to women whom she trusted. At the same time, she returned the favor to other women, taking an interest in a young Irish girl in prison, endorsing organizers of a Society for Needlewomen, inquiring into the need for a children's hospital in London, supporting a trial public nursery, and investigating a Governesses Home. Understanding the need for public support systems if women were not to be silenced by the constant demands of family or a terrifying sense of isolation, Gaskell worked, and wrote, to help put those systems in place. What Gaskell was attempting, in these engagements and others, was to create a female community, which Adrienne Rich has identified as a necessary prerequisite to creative work. Consequently, she rejected the temptation to "shut [her]self up secure from interruption in any room," deciding instead to keep herself "in readiness to give . . . sympathy or advice at any moment" (Letter 480).

In her own life, Gaskell constantly juxtaposed the public moment with the private one, writing about the composition of her latest novel alongside the purchase of a gown for a daughter, the death of the family cat, the problem of dandelions in the yard. In so doing, she was demonstrating the way that women's lives were lived out as they go about doing the work: painting the picture, writing the music, baking the bread. Both her life and her fiction testify to the truth that Adrienne Rich expressed: "We can go on trying to talk to each other, we can sometimes help each other, poetry and fiction can show us what the other is going through; but women can no longer be primarily mothers and muses for men; we have our own work cut out for us."[5]

Notes

1. Schor, *Scheherezade in the Marketplace*, 4.

2. See *Silences*, 16.

3. Ibid., 19, 33.

4. Woolf, *A Room of One's Own* in *Woman as Writer*, ed. Jeannette L. Webber and Joan Grumman, 6.

5. Rich, "When We Dead Awaken," in *Woman as Writer*, ed. Jeannette L. Webber and Joan Grumman, 132.

References

Alexander, Sally. *Women's Work in Nineteenth Century London: A Study of the Years 1820-1850*. London: Journeyman, 1983.

Altick, Richard D. *The English Common Reader: A Social History of the Mass Reading Public, 1800-1900*. Chicago: University of Chicago Press, 1957.

Auerbach, Nina. *Communities of Women: An Idea in Fiction*. Cambridge: Harvard University Press, 1978.

Basch, Françoise. *Relative Creatures: Victorian Women in Society and the Novel*. Trans. Anthony Rudolf. New York: Schocken, 1974.

Beer, Patricia. *Reader, I Married Him: A Study of the Women Characters of Jane Austen, Charlotte Brontë, Elizabeth Gaskell and George Eliot*. New York: Barnes and Noble, 1974.

Bick, Suzann. "Clouding the 'Severe Truth': Elizabeth Gaskell's Strategy in *The Life of Charlotte Brontë*." *Essays in Arts and Sciences* 11 (1982): 33-47.

Bodenheimer, Rosemarie. *The Politics of Story in Victorian Social Fiction*. Ithaca: Cornell University Press, 1988.

Bonaparte, Felicia. *The Gypsy-Bachelor of Manchester: The Life of Mrs. Gaskell's Demon*. Charlottesville: University Press of Virginia, 1992.

Bowers, Bege K., and Barbara Brothers, eds. *Reading and Writing Women's Lives: A Study of the Novel of Manners*. Ann Arbor: UMI Research Press, 1990.

Branca, Patricia. *Silent Sisterhood: Middle-Class Women in the Victorian Home*. London: Croom Helm, 1975.

Braun, Thom. *Disraeli the Novelist*. London: George Allen, 1981.

Bridenthal, Renate, and Claudia Koonz, eds. *Becoming Visible: Women in European History*. Boston: Houghton Mifflin, 1977.

Brodetsky, Tessa. *Elizabeth Gaskell*. Leamington Spa, United Kingdom: Berg, 1986.

Brontë, Charlotte. *Jane Eyre*. New York: Penguin, 1966.

____. *Villette*. Oxford: Basil Blackwell, 1931.

Brown, Gillian. *Domestic Individualism: Imagining Self in Nineteenth Century America*. Berkeley: University of California Press, 1990.

Brownstein, Rachel M. *Becoming a Heroine: Reading about Women in Novels*. New York: Viking, 1982.

Buchanan, Laurie E. "Contradicting the Ideal: The Heroines in the Novels of Elizabeth Gaskell." Dissertation. Bowling Green State University. 1985.

Burman, Sandra, ed. *Fit Work for Women*. New York: St. Martin's, 1979.

Burstyn, Joan N. *Victorian Education and the Ideal of Womanhood.* London: Croom Helm, 1980.

Calder, Jenni. *Women and Marriage in Victorian Fiction.* New York: Oxford, 1976.

Carlyle, Thomas. *Past and Present.* New York: Charles Scribner's Sons, 1899.

Casteras, Susan P. *Images of Victorian Womanhood in English Art.* Cranbury: Associated University Presses, 1987.

Cecil, David. *Victorian Novelists.* Chicago: University of Chicago Press, 1934.

Cosslett, Tess. *Woman to Woman: Female Friendship in Victorian Fiction.* Atlantic Highlands: Humanities Press, 1988.

Craik, Wendy Ann. *Elizabeth Gaskell and the English Provincial Novel.* London: Methuen, 1975.

Crosby, Christina. *The Ends of History: Victorians and 'The Woman Question.'* New York: Routledge, 1991.

Crow, Duncan. *The Victorian Woman.* New York: Stein and Day, 1971.

David, Deirdre. *Fictions of Resolution in Three Victorian Novels.* New York: Columbia University Press, 1981.

Davis, Deanna L. "Feminist Critics and Literary Mothers: Daughters Reading Elizabeth Gaskell." *Signs* 17 (1992): 507-532.

Dickens, Charles. *Hard Times.* New York: Penguin, 1978.

Disraeli, Benjamin. *Sybil, or The Two Nations.* New York: Knopf, 1934.

Du Plessis, Rachel. *Writing Beyond the Ending: Narrative Strategies of Twentieth-Century Women Writers.* Bloomington: Indiana University Press, 1985.

Dodsworth, Martin. "Women Without Men at *Cranford*." *Essays in Criticism* 13 (1963): 132-45.

Dunbar, Janet. *The Early Victorian Woman: Some Aspects of Her Life: 1837-57.* London: George G. Harrap, 1953.

Duthie, Enid L. *The Themes of Elizabeth Gaskell.* Totowa: Rowman and Littlefield, 1980.

Edwards, P. D. *Idyllic Realism from Mary Russell Mitford to Hardy.* New York: St. Martin's, 1988.

Eifrig, Gail McGrew. "Growing Out of Motherhood: The Changing Role of the Narrator in the Works of Elizabeth Gaskell." Dissertation. Bryn Mawr College. 1982.

Eliot, George. *Felix Holt the Radical.* Boston: Houghton, 1907.

_____. *Middlemarch.* New York: Penguin, 1965.

_____. *The Mill on the Floss.* New York: Penguin, 1979.

Ellis, Sarah. *The Women of England.* New York: Edward Walker, 1838.

Faber, Richard. *Proper Stations: Class in Victorian Fiction.* London: Faber and Faber, 1971.

Foster, Shirley. *Victorian Women's Fiction: Marriage, Freedom and the Individual*. Totowa: Barnes and Noble, 1985.

Gallagher, Catherine. *The Industrial Reformation of English Fiction: Social Discourse and Narrative Form, 1832-1867*. Chicago: University of Chicago Press, 1985.

Ganz, Margaret. *Elizabeth Gaskell: The Artist in Conflict*. New York: Twayne, 1969.

Gaskell, Elizabeth. *Cranford*. New York: Everyman, 1906.

____. *The Letters of Mrs. Gaskell*. Ed. J.A.V. Chapple and Arthur Pollard. Cambridge: Harvard University Press, 1967.

____. *The Life of Charlotte Brontë*. New York: Penguin, 1975.

____. *Mary Barton*. New York: Penguin, 1970.

____. *North and South*. New York: Penguin, 1970.

____. *Wives and Daughters*. New York: Penguin, 1969.

Gérin, Winifred. *Elizabeth Gaskell: A Biography*. Oxford: Clarendon, 1976.

Gilligan, Carol. *In a Different Voice: Psychological Theory and Women's Development*. Cambridge: Harvard University Press, 1982.

Gorham, Deborah. *The Victorian Girl and the Feminine Ideal*. Bloomington: Indiana University Press, 1982.

Gornick, Vivian and Barbara Moran, eds. *Woman in Sexist Society*. New York: Basic Books, 1971.

Green, Katherine Sobba. *The Courtship Novel: 1740-1820: A Feminized Genre*. Lexington: University Press of Kentucky, 1991.

Greg, W. R. "Why are Women Redundant?" *National Review* 14 (1862): 436.

Haldane, Elizabeth. *Mrs. Gaskell and Her Friends*. New York: D. Appleton, 1931.

Harman, Barbara Leah. "In Promiscuous Company: Female Public Appearance in Elizabeth Gaskell's North and South." *Victorian Studies* 31 (1988): 351-74.

Heilbrun, Carolyn G. *Writing a Woman's Life*. New York: W. W. Norton, 1988.

Holcombe, Lee. *Victorian Ladies at Work: Middle-Class Working Women in England and Wales, 1850-1914*. Washington: Archon, 1973.

Homans, Margaret. *Bearing the Word: Language and Female Experience in Nineteenth Century Women's Writing*. Chicago: University of Chicago Press, 1986.

Horn, Pamela. *Education in Rural England 1800-1914*. New York: St. Martin's, 1978.

Howell, Mary Brooks. "The Heart of Elizabeth Gaskell: The Unitarian Spirit." Dissertation. Texas Woman's University. 1985.

Hundert, Edward Joseph. "The Conception of Work and the Worker in Early Industrial England: Studies of an Ideology in Transition." Dissertation. University of Rochester. 1969.

Hunt, Linda C. *A Woman's Portion: Ideology, Culture, and the British Female Novel Tradition.* New York: Garland, 1988.

Hunter, Shelagh. *Victorian Idyllic Fiction: Pastoral Strategies.* Atlantic Highlands: Humanities Press, 1984.

Killham, John. *Tennyson and The Princess: Reflections of an Age.* London: Athlone, 1958.

Kingsley, Charles. *Alton Locke.* London: Macmillan, 1905.

Langland, Elizabeth. "Nobody's Angels: Domestic Ideology and Middle-Class Women in the Victorian Novel." *PMLA* 107 (1992): 290-304.

Lansbury, Coral. Elizabeth Gaskell. Boston: Twayne, 1984.

___. *Elizabeth Gaskell: The Novel of Social Crisis.* London: Paul Elek, 1975.

Levine, Philippa. *Feminist Lives in Victorian England: Private Roles and Public Commitment.* Oxford: Basil Blackwell, 1990.

Lewis, Jane ed. *Labour and Love: Women's Experience of Home and Family, 1850-1940.* Oxford: Basil Blackwell, 1986.

Lonoff, Sue. *Wilkie Collins and His Victorian Readers: A Study in the Rhetoric of Authorship.* New York: AMS, 1982.

Lovell, Terry. *Consuming Fiction.* New York: Verso, 1987.

Macaulay, Thomas Babington. *Southey's Colloquies on Society.* In *Literary Essays.* London: Oxford University Press, 1913.

McCully, Michael. "Beyond 'The Convent and the Cottage': A Reconsideration of Disraeli's *Sybil.*" *College Language Association* 29 (1986): 318-35.

McVeagh, John. *Elizabeth Gaskell.* New York: Humanities Press, 1970.

Martin, Carol A. "'No Angel in the House.'" *Midwest Quarterly* 24 (1983): 297-314.

Martin, Hazel T. *Petticoat Rebels: A Study of the Novels of Social Protest of George Eliot, Elizabeth Gaskell and Charlotte Brontë.* New York: Helios Books, 1968.

Martineau, Harriet. *Household Education.* Cambridge: Riverside, 1848.

Matthews, John. "Literature and Politics: A Disraelian View." *English Studies in Canada* 2 (1984): 172-87.

Miles, Rosalind. *The Female Form: Women Writers and the Conquest of the Novel.* New York: Routledge and Kegan Paul, 1987.

Mintz, Alan. *George Eliot and the Novel of Vocation.* Cambridge: Harvard University Press, 1978.

Mitchell, Sally. *The Fallen Angel: Chastity, Class and Women's Reading, 1835-1880.* Bowling Green: Bowling Green University Popular Press, 1981.

Mitford, Mary Russell. *Our Village.* London: George G. Harrap, 1947.

Nestor, Pauline. *Female Friendships and Communities*. Oxford: Clarendon, 1985.

Newton, Judith Lowder. *Women, Power, and Subversion: Social Strategies in British Fiction, 1778-1860*. Athens: University of Georgia Press, 1981.

Olsen, Tillie. *Silences*. New York: Dell, 1965.

Pichanick, Valerie Kossen. *Harriet Martineau: The Woman and Her Work, 1802-76*. Ann Arbor: University of Michigan Press, 1980.

Pinchbeck, Ivy. *Women Workers and the Industrial Revolution, 1750-1850*. London: Routledge and Sons, 1930.

Poovey, Mary. *Uneven Developments: The Ideological Work of Gender in Mid-Victorian England*. Chicago: University of Chicago Press, 1988.

Robinson, David. *Apostle of Culture: Emerson as Preacher and Lecturer*. Philadelphia: University of Pennsylvania Press, 1982.

Rodgers, Daniel T. *The Work Ethic in Industrial America, 1850-1920*. Chicago: University of Chicago Press, 1978.

Rogers, Philip. "Lessons for Fine Ladies: Tolstoy and George Eliot's Felix Holt, the Radical." *Slavic and East European Journal* 29 (1985): 379-92.

Ruskin, John. *Sesame and Lilies*. London: J. M. Dent and Sons, 1907.

Said, Edward. *The World, the Text, and the Critic*. Cambridge: Harvard University Press, 1983.

Schor, Hilary M. *Scheherazade in the Marketplace: Elizaeth Gaskell and the Victorian Novel*. New York: Oxford, 1992.

Shelston, Alan. *Biography*. London: Methuen, 1977.

Showalter, Elaine. *The New Feminist Criticism: Essays on Women, Literature and Theory*. New York: Pantheon, 1985.

____. *A Literature of Their Own: British Women Novelists from Brontë to Lessing*. Princeton: Princeton University Press, 1977.

Smith-Rosenburg, Carroll. "The Female World of Love and Ritual: Relations between Women in Nineteenth Century America." *Signs* 1 (1975): 1-25.

Spacks, Patricia Meyer. *The Female Imagination*. New York: Alfred A. Knopf, 1975.

Spencer, Jane. *Elizabeth Gaskell*. New York: St. Martin's, 1993.

Spender, Dale. *Mothers of the Novel: 100 Good Women Writers Before Jane Austen*. New York: Pandora, 1986.

Stoneman, Patsy. *Elizabeth Gaskell*. Bloomington: Indiana University Press, 1987.

Swindell, Julia. *Victorian Writing and Working Women*. Minneapolis: University of Minnesota Press, 1986.

Tennyson, Alfred Lord. *The Poetic and Dramatic Works of Alfred Lord Tennyson*. New York: Houghton Mifflin, 1899.

Tillotson, Kathleen. *Novels of the Eighteen Forties*. Oxford: Clarendon, 1954.

Uglow, Jenny. *Elizabeth Gaskell*. New York: Farrar, Straus, Giroux, 1993.

Vicinus, Martha, ed. *Suffer and Be Still: Women in the Victorian Age*. Bloomington: Indiana University Press, 1972.

___. *A Widening Sphere: Changing Roles of Victorian Women*. Bloomington: Indiana University Press, 1977.

Webber, Jeannette L., and Joan Grumman, eds. *Woman as Writer*. Boston: Houghton Mifflin, 1978.

Weiss, Barbara. "Elizabeth Gaskell: The Telling of Feminine Tales." *Studies in the Novel* 16 (1984): 274-87.

Williams, Merryn. *Women in the English Novel, 1800-1900*. New York: St. Martin's, 1984.

Williams, Raymond. *Culture and Society 1780-1950*. London: Chalto and Windus, 1958.

Wohl, Anthony S., ed. *The Victorian Family, Structure and Stresses*. New York: St. Martin's, 1978.

Wolfe, Patricia A. "Structure and Movement in Cranford." *Nineteenth Century Fiction* 23 (1968): 161-76.

Woodbury, Lynn. "Elizabeth Gaskell and the Victorian Outsider: A Study of My Diary: the Early Years of My Daughter Marianne, Mary Barton and Ruth." Dissertation. University of California. 1983.

Wright, Edgar. *Mrs. Gaskell: The Basis for Reassessment*. London: Oxford, 1965.

Yeazell, Ruth. "Why Political Novels Have Heroines: Sybil, Mary Barton, and Felix Holt." *Novel* 18 (1985): 126-144.

Index

About the Author

ROBIN B. COLBY is Assistant Professor of English at Meredith College, Raleigh, N.C.

ISBN 0-313-29373-2

90000>

EAN

9 780313 293733

HARDCOVER BAR CODE